The Investors Tax Tuneup

The Investors Tax Tuneup

It's What You *Keep* That Counts

Edward A. Lyon, JD

Authors Choice Press

San Jose New York Lincoln Shanghai

The Investors Tax Tuneup
It's What You Keep That Counts

Authors Choice Press
an imprint of iUniverse.com, Inc.

For information address:
iUniverse.com, Inc.
5220 S 16th, Ste. 200
Lincoln, NE 68512
www.iuniverse.com

This publication is designed to provide accurate and authoritative information in regard to the subject matter covered. It is sold with the understanding that the publisher is not engaged in rendering legal, accounting, or other professional service. If legal advice or other expert assistance is required, the services of a competent professional should be sought. - From a Declaration of Principles jointly adopted by a Committee of the American Bar Association and a Committee of Publishers and Association.

ISBN: 0-595-15193-0

Printed in the United States of America

*This book is dedicated to Mary, Molly, Mary Claire, and Margaret—
my four priceless deductions.*

Contents

Chapter 1

It's What You *Keep* That Counts

If you invest, you pay taxes. No matter what you buy, every investment you make has some effect or another on your taxes. You can wrap them in qualified plans, IRAs, and annuities. But someday, someone has to pay. Even supposedly tax-free municipal bonds affect alternative minimum tax, Social Security, and estate tax. It may be true, as Supreme Court Justice Oliver Wendell Holmes said, that taxes are the price we pay for civilization. But are we really so civilized that we should pay up to half of our incomes in taxes?

As an investor, you face two main hurdles to maximizing your returns: taxes and expenses. Both attack your investments because both, like interest, compound over time. When you pay a dollar of taxes or fees on your investments, you don't just lose the dollar you pay. You lose all the income that dollar could have generated in the future. But taxes attack your investments harder because taxes take a bigger bite. Jeremy Siegel, author of *Stocks for the Long Run*, has calculated the damage taxes wreak on investment results. His study looked at growth from 1801 to 1997:

- A dollar invested in bonds grew to $727 before taxes—but just $73 after taxes. That's barely 10% of the pre-tax total.
- A dollar invested in tax-free municipal bonds did slightly better, growing to $413.
- A dollar invested in stocks grew to an impressive $514,605 before taxes—but just $23,684 after taxes. That's an insulting 4.6% of the pre-tax total.

The real tragedy is that you can avoid these tax bills entirely. The solution is tax-efficient investing—the search for the best *after-tax* return. Tax-efficient investing is a new challenge. You'll have to rethink some of your most basic assumptions about your investments. But the rewards will multiply your wealth. That's because you have more control over your taxes than you do with any other investment choice. It doesn't matter whether you're a novice investor deferring $100 a month into a 401(k) or a seasoned veteran with a million-dollar portfolio. You can arrange your investments to avoid paying a single dime of tax. In 1997, 1,781 of the richest Americans did just that. These lucky winners all earned over $200,000—and paid nothing in federal income tax. 36,759 more made over $200,000 and paid less than 15% tax. This book tells you how they did it—and how you can too.

1.1   Tax System Overview

Before we dive into investments, let's briefly discuss how the tax system works. You'll need to know how your investment choices affect figures such as gross income, adjusted gross income, taxable income, and the like. So it's important to define these concepts before we discuss how to control them. Here, in a nutshell, is how the tax system works.

First, add up your taxable income from all sources to determine your total income.

Taxable income includes most of what we think of as income:

- wages, salaries, and tips
- commissions

- profit from business
- interest and dividends
- capital gains from the sale of property
- pension and annuity proceeds
- rents and royalties
- alimony received
- gambling winnings, lotteries, and Who Wants to be a Millionaire?
- barter
- some employee benefits
- illegal income

Taxable income doesn't include every last dollar you take in. Make sure you don't enrich the Treasury with taxes on income you don't have to report:

- gifts and inheritances
- loans
- most life insurance proceeds and dividends
- municipal bond interest
- rollover IRAs
- property settlements
- child-support payments
- damages from some lawsuits
- workers' compensation benefits
- disability insurance proceeds (if you paid the premiums yourself)
- federal tax refunds
- state tax refunds (if you didn't itemize the previous year)
- most scholarships and settlements

Next, subtract adjustments to income to determine adjusted gross income.

Adjustments to income are a group of specific deductions that cut your tax by cutting your taxable income. These include:

- IRA contributions
- moving expenses
- one-half of self-employment tax paid
- self-employed health insurance
- Keogh and Simplified Employee Pension (SEP) contributions
- penalty on early withdrawal of savings
- alimony paid
- student loan interest

Total income minus adjustments to income equals adjusted gross income, or AGI. This total is important for two reasons:

- Your personal exemptions and itemized deductions phase out as your adjusted gross income reaches certain levels. Personal exemptions shrink by 2% for each $2,500 or fraction over the threshold. Itemized deductions (except for medical expenses, investment interest, casualty and theft losses, and gambling losses) shrink by 3% for each dollar over the threshold, up to a maximum of 80% of total itemized deductions. For 1999, personal exemptions start phasing out at $126,600 for single filers, $158,300 for heads of households, $189,950 for joint filers, and $94,975 for married couples filing separately. Itemized deductions start phasing out at $126,600 for single filers, heads of households, and joint filers, and $63,300 for married couples filing separately.
- Many itemized deductions, such as medical expenses are allowed only to the extent they exceed certain percentages of adjusted gross income. Medical expenses are deductible only to the extent they top 7.5% of adjusted gross income; casualty and theft losses are deductible only to the extent they exceed $100 plus 10% of adjusted gross income; and miscellaneous itemized deductions are allowed only to the extent they

exceed 2% of adjusted gross income. If your adjusted gross income is $50,000, you can deduct medical expenses only over $3,750. If you have just $3,500 of medical expenses, you're out of luck.

Next, subtract deductions and personal exemptions to determine taxable income.

Itemized deductions are the classic writeoffs most of us think of as "tax deductions." These include:

- medical expenses
- state, local, and foreign taxes
- interest
- casualty and theft losses
- charitable gifts
- miscellaneous itemized deductions (tax preparation fees, investment expenses, etc.)

Itemized deductions grow more valuable as your tax increases. If you're in the 15% bracket, every dollar you deduct cuts your tax by 15 cents. If you're in the 39.6% bracket, that same dollar deduction cuts your tax by 39.6 cents.

The starting point for every taxpayer is the standard deduction: $4,300 for single filers; $6,350 for heads of households; $7,200 for joint filers; and $3,600 for married couples filing separately (1999). If your actual itemized deductions are higher than the standard deduction, take your itemized total; if actual deductions are lower, take the standard deduction. (Married couples filing separately must both itemize or both take the standard deduction; you can't have it both ways.) Standard deductions are high enough that less than one out of three taxpayers itemize deductions. There's no magic to using them other than knowing what's out there.

Personal exemptions are deductions you get for yourself, your spouse, and each dependent. A dependent is someone who gets more than half of their support from you, and meets certain other tests. Each personal exemption cuts your adjusted gross income by $2,750. Dependents qualify if they:

- are your child, stepchild, grandchild, parent or stepparent, sibling or stepsibling, in-law, aunt/uncle, niece/nephew, or anyone else not breaking state law by living with you (in some states, same-sex couples can declare each other dependents),
- earn less than $2,650 in taxable income (not including Social Security, tax-exempt interest, etc.), except for children under age 19 or full-time students under age 24,
- get more than half their support from you,
- are a U.S. citizen, U.S. resident, or resident of Canada or Mexico, and
- don't file a joint return with his or her spouse (except where each spouse's income is below the filing threshold and they file to claim a refund).

You'll need to provide a Social Security number for each dependent you claim. A dependent doesn't have to be alive for a full year to qualify for the full personal exemption. Children born during the year and people who die during the year qualify for personal exemptions. (If you have a foster child and your actual expenses top the allowance you get from the state, claim the excess as an itemized deduction.)

Consult the tax tables or table of tax brackets to determine your tax.

Our "progressive" system is designed to gather the most tax from those of us most able to pay. That means that the percentage of income you pay increases with your income. Tax brackets govern the amount of tax you pay on each dollar of income. Your "tax bracket" is the percentage you pay on your last dollar of income. 1999 tax brackets for various filers are:

1999 Tax Brackets	
Single Filers: $0 - $25,350 15% $25,351 - $61,400 28% $61,401 - $128,100 31% $128,101 - $278,450 36% $278,451+ 39.6%	**Married Filing Jointly:** $0 - $42,350 15% $42,351 - $102,300 28% $102,301 - $155,950 31% $155,951 - $278,450 36% $278,451+ 39.6%
Heads of Households: $0 - $33,950 15% $33,951 - $87,700 28% $87,701 - $142,000 31% $142,001 - $278,450 36% $278,451+ 39.6%	**Married Filing Separately:** $0 - $21,175 15% $21,176 - $51,150 28% $51,151 - $77,975 31% $77,976 - $139,225 36% $139,226+ 39.6%

There's one crucial exception to these tables. Long-term capital gains (gains from the sale of property held for more 12 months) are generally taxed at no more than 20%, even if your regular tax bracket is far higher. Lower long-term capital gains rates are the single best opportunity for investors to cut their taxes. We'll return to this strategy throughout the *Toolkit*.

You'll also need to add in any extra taxes, such as self-employment tax or alternative minimum tax (AMT). The AMT is especially vicious. You calculate it by taking your regular taxable income, then adding "preferences" and "adjustments" like certain tax-free bond interest, the portion of medical deductions between 7.5% and 10.0% of AGI, and other items too frightening for most taxpayers to consider. If AMT calculated on that income is higher than regular tax, then you pay the higher amount.

Don't forget state and local taxes, too!

Finally, subtract any available tax credits and send a check to the IRS.

Tax credits are like turbocharged tax deductions, only better. Tax deductions cut your taxable income. Every dollar of deduction cuts your tax by whatever percentage of that deduction equals your tax bracket. Every dollar of credit cuts your tax by a full dollar.

Tax deductions grow more valuable as your taxable income rises. As we discussed earlier, if you're in the 15% bracket, every dollar you deduct cuts your tax by 15 cents. If you're in the 39.6% bracket, that same dollar deduction cuts your tax by 39 cents. But tax credits are more valuable for taxpayers in lower brackets. In the 39.6% bracket, you'd need $2,525 in deductions to get the same break as a $1,000 deduction. In the 15% bracket, you'd need a whopping $6,666.66 in deductions to equal that $1,000 credit.

There's no shortage of tax credits you can use to cut that final bill. Most of them have no particular connection to your investments. However, we'll discuss the final two when we cover real estate:

- adoption tax credit
- child tax credit
- dependent care credit
- earned income tax credit
- elderly and disabled tax credit
- foreign tax credit
- Hope Scholarship tax credit
- Lifetime Learning tax credit
- *low-income housing tax credit*
- *rehabilitation tax credit*

That's really most of what you need to know. The real issue isn't the numbers. It's what you have to include in your income, what you get to deduct from that income, and where you invest to avoid reporting income at all.

Given how the tax system works, then, there are three main ways to keep down your tax:

Buy Tax-Advantaged Investments That Don't Increase Your Income

You have more control over your investments than any other aspect of your return. For example, you can buy municipal bonds that pay tax-free income. You can invest inside tax-deferred wrappers that defer gains until you sell. And you can buy investments that reward you with lower-taxed long-term capital gains. The bulk of this *Toolkit* discusses these choices.

Make the Most of Adjustments to Income, Deductions, and Credits

Adjustments to income and deductions cut your tax bill by cutting your taxable income. You may be amazed to discover how much you can already deduct. This *Toolkit* will show you how.

Shift Income to Other Taxpayers and Other Tax Years

If you can shift income from this year's return to next year's, you'll cut this year's tax. It's valuable even if it just let's you squeeze another year's use out of your tax dollar. You've probably heard that "justice delayed is justice denied." Well, a tax bill delayed is a tax cut. And if you can shift income to a lower-bracket taxpayer, such as a retired parent or a child, you'll do even better.

1.2   Investment Decisions/Tax Decisions

This isn't a tax book about investments. I won't tell you how to file Schedules B and D. I won't show you how to calculate original issue discount on zero-coupon Treasuries. And I won't walk you through the Modified Accelerated Cost Recovery System schedules that defer taxes on equipment leasing deals. There are plenty of outstanding tax planning and preparation guides to help with those questions.

This is an *investment* book about *taxes*. Some investment books tell you how to invest for retirement. Others cover general investing principles. Still more programs cover specific investment strategies such as contrarian investing, technology, the dogs of the Dow^{sm}, and international stocks. The *Toolkit* helps you make more money by investing tax-efficiently.

Investment pros will tell you never to make investment decisions for tax reasons. The 1980s tax shelter disaster is a glaring warning against letting tax considerations drive investment choices. Thousands of investors sank billions of dollars into real estate and energy limited partnerships, cattle breeding and feeding arrangements, master recordings, and other schemes, not because they were appropriate investments, but because the tax code let them write off more than their actual investment. When Congress pulled the plug in 1986, tax shelters slid down the drain, sucking thousands of hapless victims along with them.

I agree that fundamental factors of risk and reward are the place to start with planning your investments. Let's quickly identify some of the issues you need to consider *before* you think about taxes—and, more important, how to answer them:

• Asset allocation—the percentages of your portfolio that you allocate to equities, bonds, and cash—accounts for the largest part of your long-term investment return. This is an outgrowth of Nobel Prize-winning Modern Portfolio Theory. The process involves balancing different types of investments to lower your overall portfolio risk. One influential study found that that asset allocation controls as much as 93.6% of your investment return, with security selection accounting for just 4.2% and market timing accounting for just 1.7% more. (Brinson, Hood, and Beebower, "Determinants of Portfolio Performance," Financial Analysts Journal, July-August, 1986.) Although these precise figures have been challenged, there is widespread consensus that asset allocation is the engine that drives your investment performance.

Asset allocation is as much an art as a science. You can find portfolio "optimizers" to craft a portfolio designed to give you the highest possible return for the amount of risk you're willing to assume (or, conversely, the lowest possible risk for a given return). But these solutions can be impractical—for example, one might recommend unrealistically large allocations to asset classes such as junk bonds or commodities. And optimizers are based on historical data. Yesterday's data shapes today's projections, which may bear little relationship to tomorrow's results. The best programs rely on a theory dubbed "Post-Modern Portfolio Theory" to measure your chances of reaching a particular goal. They use a statistical tool called Monte Carlo analysis to run thousands of trials, then project your chance of accomplishing your stated goals.

• Style analysis describes the specific characteristics of each investment you buy. For fixed income investments, style dimensions include interest-rate sensitivity and default risk. For stocks, style dimensions include size and value. For international stocks, style also includes country exposure. Developed markets like Europe and Japan affect your portfolio differently than emerging markets (Wall Street marketing jargon for "speculative former third-world crap").

Style analysis, like asset allocation, is an art as well as a science. It turns as much on your temperament as much as your objectives. Do you like to ride the market like a cowboy on a bull? If so, invest as aggressively as you can in small, growth-oriented stocks and funds. Look for companies you've never heard of and countries that don't make the evening news. Do market fluctuations make you nervous? If so, choose steadier, conservative large-cap and value targets.

- Once you've decided which asset classes and investment styles to use, you'll need to choose between individual securities and managed money. Mutual funds and separate accounts offer professional management and instant diversification at a reasonable price. These are obvious advantages for new investors and for specialized asset classes such as junk bonds. But even if you prefer to pick your holdings yourself, you may not be able to create and maintain a diversified portfolio for less than it costs to buy and own a fund.

    The rule here is simple: if it would cost you more in commissions, spreads, and other costs to build and manage a properly diversified portfolio, then buy a fund. You can always start with mutual funds as core holdings and add individual securities as your portfolio grows. Let's say you'd have $20,000 to allocate to large-cap stocks. An inexpensive index fund or exchange-traded fund would cost less than 0.20%, or $40, per year. You probably can't assemble a portfolio of sufficiently diversified individual stocks for less—so your best bet is the fund. Once you have $100,000, you can economically diversify, or hire a private portfolio manager who can run your money with an eye to your own tax situation.

- Finally, consider costs, convenience, and service. Do you value the service you get from a money manager, financial planner, or full-service broker? If so, that service should justify fees and commissions you pay manage your portfolio.

    I'm a former stockbroker and a registered investment advisor. I can certainly manage my own money. But I still use a full-service broker for a valuable second opinion. And psychologically, using an advisor keeps me from beating myself up over each and every decision.

If you choose to work with an advisor, choose one who's licensed to help you take advantage of the full range of investment products you'll need. Most insurance agents and many financial planners are "Series 6" registered representatives. This means they can supply mutual funds, variable life insurance, and variable annuities. They can help you take advantage of index funds and tax-managed mutual funds. (See Chapter Four.) Full-service stockbrokers and financial planners are "Series 7" licensed. They can supply everything a Series 6 registered representative, can, along with individual stocks and bonds, exchange-traded funds, and separate accounts. If you have large taxable amounts to invest, you're probably better off with a Series 7 registered rep who can supply a fuller range of tax-advantaged products.

If you like to run the show yourself, find inexpensive discount brokers that charge for what you need, not more. Consider doing business over the Internet, which offers even lower fees, along with a wealth of information previously limited to the Wall Street pros themselves. But be aware that what's in your discount broker's best interest—namely, commissionable transactions—may not be in your best interest. They make money whether you do or not. Don't fall prey to their not-so-subtle suggestion that low fees and frequent trading are the road to riches.

Having said all that, in the end, it's what you *keep* that counts. Your quick killing on a hot Internet stock looks a lot less impressive after the federal, state, and local tax men confiscate half of your gain. If you don't plan carefully, you'll find that the IRS is your partner in every investment you make. *Once you've decided what move to make, your next step should be to find the most tax-efficient way to make it.* That is the purpose of this *Toolkit.*

Choosing tax-efficient investments pays dividends throughout your portfolio. For starters, it's easy! It's hard to beat the market—that's why so few investment managers do it. But it's easy to beat the tax collector. Tax-efficient investing gives you more control over your net returns, even in a down market. That's because you decide when to pay the bill. What's more, tax-efficient investing guarantees tax-efficient results. Why roll the dice on a hot dot.com stock when you can count on the tax code to give you a break? You can't control investments. You *can* control taxes. And small increases in tax efficiency pay huge gains over time.

Finally, choosing tax-advantaged investments does more than just cut your tax on your investments. It cuts your taxes throughout your entire return. Consider these additional plusses of tax-advantaged investments:

- As we discussed earlier, many deductions are available only after they top a certain percentage of your adjusted gross income. Extra taxable income wipes out those deductions. So the extra investment income doesn't just cost you the tax you pay on the investment income—it also costs you the extra tax you pay when the income erases your deductions.
- As we also discussed, your itemized deductions and personal exemptions phase out as your AGI tops a certain level. Once again, extra investment income it doesn't just cost you the tax you pay on the income—it also costs you the extra tax you pay when the income erases your deductions.
- Some tax breaks simply vanish once your AGI tops certain levels. For example, you can't contribute to a Roth IRA if you make more than $110,000 ($160,000 for joint filers). Keeping your investment income down preserves these valuable breaks.
- Most investments increase tax you pay on your Social Security benefits. Those benefits are tax-free unless your provisional income tops certain levels. But this figure includes income from nearly all your investments—even supposedly tax-free municipal bonds!

These various phaseouts can combine in different ways for each tax-payer. Your true marginal rate (the rate you pay on your last dollar of income) can be far different than the five tax brackets: 15%, 28%, 31%, 36%, and 39.6%. Your rate can even vary for different types of income.

You can use a tax prep program like Intuit's *TurboTax*, Kiplinger's *TaxCut*, or Microsoft's TaxSaver to discover your true rate. Enter your data to give yourself a picture of your current situation. Then enter another $100 of income in various places to see how it affects your bottom line. Enter $100 of taxable bond income, then $100 of tax-free municipal bond income. Add $100 of stock dividends and $100 of long-term capital gain. If you collect Social Security, add $100 of municipal bond income to see how it affects taxing your Social Security. If you buy Treasuries, make sure you buy the state module to see the effect of state tax-free interest. Next, see just how much a $100 deduction saves you. You might be surprised to find that your deduction saves you far less than your published marginal rate. (Don't forget to deduct the the program!)

In the end, your goal shouldn't be to pay the least tax. Your real goal should be to earn the highest *after-tax* return consistent with your investment objectives. This means you'll have to consider your risk tolerance along with objective tax planning advice. The most tax-efficient way to invest may be to find the next Microsoft—a hot growth stock with no dividend—and simply hang on for the ride. It worked for Microsoft founder Bill Gates, and he's the richest man in America. But Gates has seen his stock's value plummet by billions in a single day. Can you stomach that kind of volatility? If not, find tax-advantaged investments you can sleep with.

1.3   Paying Less/Paying Later

Before we dive into tax-cutting strategies, we need to look at a fundamental choice that governs every investment decision you make. There are really just two ways you can invest your money—*loan* or *own*. You can loan your money, in the form of cash equivalents, such as bank deposits and money market funds, or in the form of bonds, which are negotiable promissory notes. Or you can own your investments, by buying stocks, real estate, commodities, collectibles, or "derivatives" based on the price of some other underlying asset.

- Loaning produces ordinary income, such as interest and dividends. You pay tax on this income, as you earn it, at regular rates. You can also earn capital gains or losses if the value of your outstanding loan rises or falls. (This can happen with changes in interest rates or the borrower's credit quality.) But the primary goal is current income.
- Owning produces capital gains, such as profits on the sale of a stock. You pay tax on these gains only when you sell. You can also earn current income from your equity investments, such as stock dividends or real estate rents. But the primary goal is capital gain.

Together, current income and capital gain produce total return, the measure of an investment's profit or loss. They also govern tax efficiency. Current income and short-term gains are less efficient than long-term capital gain. That's because current income and short-term gains are taxed today, as you receive them, at ordinary income rates. Long-term capital gain is taxed tomorrow, when you sell, at lower rates. The key to measuring tax efficiency is the portion of total return that comes from current income and short-term gain versus the portion of total return that comes from long-term gain. And this, in turn, depends on the portion of your total return that comes from loaning versus the portion of your total return that comes from owning.

This fundamental relationship suggests two ways to cut tax on our investments: pay less and pay later. Let's take a quick look at these broad categories.

1.3.1 Pay Less

For most investors, long-term capital gains are the first place to look for lower tax on your investments. These are gains from the sale of property held for more than 12 months. They actually let you pay less *and* pay later. Here's how:

- Long-term capital gains are taxed at lower rates than ordinary income—just 10% for income that would otherwise be taxed at 15% and 20% for income that would otherwise be taxed at 28% and above.
- You don't pay tax until you realize your gain (actually sell your property). This lets you decide when to pay the tax.
- If you hold appreciated property until your death, you avoid income tax entirely. Your heirs inherit the property with a cost basis (see below) equal to its value on your date of death. This stepped-up basis is an important tax and estate-planning tool: probably half of all long-term capital gains escape taxes this way.

Your capital gain on a sale is equal to your adjusted sale price minus your basis. Adjusted sale price equals your actual proceeds, minus the cost of selling the property. So, your adjusted sale price for stock equals the sale price minus the commission. Your adjusted sale price for rental real estate equals your sale price, minus the commission and any other closing costs. Basis equals the price you pay, plus the cost of buying it, plus the cost of any improvements. So, your basis in stock is the price you pay plus the commission you pay to buy it. Your basis in rental real estate is the price you pay, plus the costs of buying it, plus any improvements you make.

The Taxpayer Relief Act of 1997 shook up the entire capital gains structure. Previously, long-term capital gains were taxed at ordinary rates for taxpayers in the 15% and 28% tax brackets. Since less than 5% of taxpayers paid more than 28%, this structure effectively denied any long-term capital gains relief to the vast majority of taxpayers. The new law extends lower rates to everyone who earns long-term capital gains. Today, you'll pay 20% on gains that previously would have been taxed at 28%, and just 10% on gains that previously would have been taxed at 15%. Beginning in 2001, you'll pay 8% on property that you've held more than five years that otherwise would have been taxed at 15%. Beginning in 2006, you'll pay 18% on property you buy after December 31, 2000, and hold five years that otherwise would be taxed at 20%. These changes extend relief to a whole new universe of taxpayers. They make capital-gains planning a crucial part of tax planning for investors whose incomes previously weren't high enough to benefit. It complicates planning, but the rewards are worth it.

There are also investments that let you pay less tax on your current income:

- Some investments pay tax-free income. For example, municipal bonds are free from federal and most state income taxes; Treasury securities are free from state taxes; and some U.S. Savings Bonds are tax-free if redeemed to pay college costs.
- Some investments give you special deductions that you can write off against income. For example, real estate gives you depreciation deductions; and oil and gas investments let you deduct intangible drilling and development costs, depreciation, and a special depletion allowance.

- Family tax planning lets you shift investments and their income to lower-bracket taxpayers, such as your children. These strategies can also save estate tax.

1.3.2 Pay Later

There are three main tools to let you pay later:

- As we've already seen, long-term capital gains treatment lets you delay tax until you sell the asset and recognize gain.
- Qualified retirement plans and IRAs shelter your gains until you take out your money. Most of these also give you an up-front deduction for your contribution.
- Life insurance and annuities let you defer tax until you withdraw your money. (In fact, permanent life insurance policies let you take advantage of your gains in the form of loans and escape tax entirely.)

But tax-deferred wrappers have three big problems:

- First, all income from these accounts is taxed at ordinary rates, regardless of the character of the underlying investment. This kills your chance to profit from lower long-term capital gains rates discussed above.
- Second, there's no opportunity for stepped-up basis at death, as there is with long-term capital gains in taxable accounts.
- Third, most withdrawals before age 59½ are subject to a 10% penalty tax.

You might think that tax-deferred accounts let you throw away the rules because you pay tax on withdrawals instead of gains. But you can't forget the rules completely. That's because you have to identify which investments benefit more from paying less and which benefit more from paying later. Remember, your real goal isn't just to avoid tax. Your real goal should be to maximize after-tax return.

1.4   Commandments of Tax-Efficient Investing

Now that I've laid down the ground rules, I'll lay out three commandments of tax-efficient investing. The rest of this course will tell you how to follow them to your greatest advantage:

1. It's what you keep that counts.
2. Once you've decided what move to make, find the most tax-efficient way to make it.
3. Never make an investment decision solely for tax reasons.

Now let's get started!

Chapter 2

Fixed Income

Fixed income investments promise a fixed rate of income for a fixed period of time. These include a wide variety of cash equivalents and bonds. Their main tax characteristic is current income.

A bond is a negotiable promissory note promising the return of a specified principal. The issuer pays a stated interest and, at the end of the term, repays the principal. There are literally thousands of bond issues available. Government issues range from the U.S. Treasury to local agencies. Corporate bonds range from blue-chip giants to Internet start-ups. And foreign issues range from super-safe British gilts to speculative paper issued by former third-world colonies.

The two main style dimensions of bond investments are credit risk and interest-rate sensitivity. Both of these affect your after-tax return:

- Credit risk is the risk that the borrower won't make interest or principal payments. For example, U.S. Treasuries are backed by the full faith and credit of the United States Treasury. They have the lowest credit risk in the world. (If the U.S. government ever defaults, the only investments worth holding will be canned goods and shotguns.) In contrast, junk bonds issued by an internet startup carry no guarantee that the issuer can actually pay the periodic interest, let alone the principal. Generally, bonds with higher credit risk pay more of their total return in the form of capital gains.
- Interest rate sensitivity is the risk that the price of your bond will rise and fall with interest rates. Long-term bonds fluctuate more than short-term bonds. Bonds with longer maturities generally pay more of their

total return in the form of capital gains because their values swing more with interest rate changes.

Bonds aren't tax-efficient because most of their total return comes from current interest, taxed immediately when you receive it. (Some bonds get special breaks that shelter some or all of their interest income. Municipal bond interest is free from federal income tax. Treasury bonds pay interest that's free from state and local tax. And U.S. Savings Bonds let you defer tax until the bond matures.) But current interest isn't the only tax consideration with a bond. That's because bond prices rise and fall as interest rates rise and fall. These price swings can generate capital gains when you sell the bond or it matures. A bond's total return consists of its annual income plus or minus capital gain or loss. Since interest income is taxed today at ordinary rates, the greater the portion of total return that comes from current income, the less efficient the bond is. Generally, short- and intermediate-term bonds pay most of their total return in current income; long-term bonds pay more in capital gain.

Bond investing is more than finding the highest yield, or even the highest after-tax return. It's about finding the highest after-tax total return. And your best choice in bonds depends on your own tax rate as much as it does on the bonds' interest income. Let's look at three different bond buyers to see how personal tax rates affect the choice. Each buyer has four available choices (returns are from *The Wall Street Journal*, November 28, 1997):

- High-yield corporate bonds pay the highest pre-tax return at 8.46%. These are subject to federal and state taxes.
- Long-term investment-grade corporate bonds pay the next highest pre-tax return at 6.78%. These are also subject to federal and state taxes.
- Long-term Treasury bonds pay 6.04%. These are subject to federal taxes only.

- Finally, long-term municipal bonds pay the lowest pre-tax at 5.31%. These are free from both federal and state taxes.

Now we'll look at three bond buyers:

- Buyer One lives in California, with a 31% federal rate and a 10% state rate yielding a combined rate of 37.9%
- Buyer Two lives in Ohio, with a 28% federal rate and a 6% state rate yielding a combined rate of 32.32%
- Buyer Three lives in Florida, with a 15% federal rate and no state income tax.

Bond Yield Comparison				
Category	Pre-tax Yield	California After-tax Yield	Ohio After-tax Yield	Florida After-tax Yield
High-Yield Corporates	8.46%	5.25%	5.73%	7.19%
Long-Term Corporates	6.75%	4.21%	4.59%	5.76%
Long-Term Treasuries	6.04%	4.17%	4.35%	5.13%
Long-Term Municipals	5.31%	5.31%	5.31%	5.31%

The California buyer nets the most with the municipal bond. The Ohio buyer does best with the junk bond. The Florida buyer does even better with the junk bond than the Ohio buyer. And those figures just reflect current yield. They don't consider capital appreciation. So you need to look at your own tax results before you buy your bonds.

Before we look at the different tax rules for different bond issuers, let's first look at tax rules for some aspects of bond investing that can apply to all issuers. There are three "twists" that can affect a bond's tax efficiency, regardless of the issuer. These include bond premiums and discounts, zero-coupon bonds, and adjustable rate bonds.

If you buy a bond at a premium—a price above its face value—you'll lose money when the bond matures. That's because the issuer won't return your full purchase price. So the IRS gives you a break for the loss you take on the premium. You can deduct it as a capital loss when the bond matures. Or you can amortize it over the life of the bond. If you amortize, you can deduct a portion of the premium against that year's interest income. To amortize a premium, simply divide the premium by the time remaining to maturity (or call date). Report your amortization on Schedule B where you report the income from the bond.

Let's say you pay $1,040 for a four-year Treasury note paying $80 per year. Your premium is $40, which, divided by four years, gives you $10 of amortization per year. You can choose to take a $40 loss when the bond matures. Or you can choose to amortize $10 and report just $70 of income per year. If you choose to amortize the premium, then sell the bond after two years, your basis for figuring gain or loss will be $1,020. So, if you sell the bond for $1,030, you'll report a $10 gain and not a $10 loss.

(If you buy municipal bonds at a premium, there's no deduction for amortization. That's because the interest isn't taxable to begin with. However, you'll have to amortize the premium for figuring any capital gain or loss on a later sale.)

Similar rules apply if you buy a bond at a discount from its final face value. In that case, any eventual gain will be taxed as capital gain. You can choose to add a portion of the gain to your annual interest income and pay tax at ordinary rates on this gain. However, it's usually more profitable to wait until you dispose of the bond, through sale, call, or maturity, then pay tax at lower capital gains rates.

Zero-coupon bonds don't pay actual interest. The issuer sells the bond at a deep discount to face value, and the bond's value rises as it moves towards maturity, finally maturing at face value. In some cases, the issuer sells a zero-coupon bond directly. In other cases, a broker strips the coupon from a regular bond and sells the principal and coupons separately. You pay tax each year on the original issue discount (OID)—the interest accreted—even though you don't get any cash. (Where's the fun in that?)

Your broker or the bond issuer will report the amount of OID to include on your return with Form 1099-OID. However, if you bought the bond at a premium (more than the total of the issue price plus all accumulated OID), or your zero-coupon is a stripped bond or coupon, you'll have to adjust the amount reported using complicated rules set forth in ***IRS Publication 1212.***

Each year, as you report OID, you add that amount to your basis for figuring gain or loss on a sale. If you sell a zero-coupon bond before maturity, you'll owe separate taxes on the portions representing the current year's income and the cumulative capital gain.

Zero-coupon bond prices move dramatically as interest rates rise and fall. Aggressive investors can use zeroes to bet on interest rates, and there are several investment strategies based on buying and selling zeroes according to economic conditions. For example, one strategy calls for you to buy one-year Treasuries when you expect rates to rise and 30-year zero coupons when you expect rates to fall. But the immediate tax bill on phantom income, along with complicated rules for figuring how much income to report each year, make these most appropriate for tax-deferred accounts.

Finally, adjustable rate bonds pay an interest rate tied to some underlying benchmark: the prime rate, Treasuries, LIBOR (the London Inter-Bank Offering Rate), or the like. Adjustable rates cut interest rate risk because, if interest rates rise, you'll get the benefit of the higher rates. At the same time, if interest rates fall, so does your income.

Since adjustable rate bond interest adjusts with interest rate swings, it naturally follows that they suffer fewer price swings as interest rates move up and down. This affects tax efficiency because adjustable rate securities pay far less of their total return, if any, in the form of capital gains. (Many junk bonds pay adjustable rates; these bonds may generate capital gains and losses if their prices rise and fall in reaction to credit quality.)

2.1 Cash

Cash and cash equivalents include piggy banks, greenbacks under the mattress, bank deposits, and money market funds. Cash is an essential part of most investors' asset allocations, as an anchor to limit portfolio volatility and a safe harbor from choppy markets. But cash has historically paid the least return over time, and cash is the least tax-efficient investment.

Bank savings accounts are the simplest cash equivalents. They pay lousy interest rates. The interest is immediately taxable. And there's not even much reward for shopping rates. The extra ¼% you might earn on a $10,000 balance (a fat $25 per year) doesn't justify the time it takes to fill out the papers to move your account. Life's just too short. Savings accounts are fine for teaching your kids to save. But we're grown-ups now, so we can ignore them.

Bank CDs are the next step up the investment ladder. The bank pays you a guaranteed rate for a fixed length of time. Interest is taxable as ordinary income immediately as it is credited. (You can use short-term CDs to defer income from one calendar year to the next if the interest isn't credited until the close of the term.) CDs promise absolute safety from Federal Deposit Insurance Corporation (FDIC) or Federal Savings and Loan Insurance Corporation (FSLIC) insured deposits. But CDs pay lousy interest, and FDIC insurance is actually less valuable than the full faith and credit of the U.S. government you get with U.S. Treasuries.

Most investors choose money market mutual funds for their cash equivalent. These funds buy short-term corporate and government paper, short-term certificates of deposit, bankers' acceptances, and repurchase agreements. Maturities are limited to 90 days. Their goal is to pay the highest possible return consistent with stable asset value and instant liquidity. There are three main classes of money market funds:

- General money market funds—those that buy a mix of corporate and government paper—are taxable immediately at your marginal rate. A fund that buys Treasury securities will report the portion of income earned from Treasury obligations exempt from state tax.
- Treasury money funds invest exclusively in Treasury securities for safety. These funds have the added advantage of being free from state income tax.
- Tax-free money market funds buy short-term municipal paper. These are free from federal income tax. They may also be fully or partially free from state income tax as well, depending on whether you buy a national fund or a single state fund. (See Chapter 2.3, "Municipal Bonds.")

Stashing Your Cash

There are plenty of tax-advantaged places to stash your cash. There's no law that says you have to hold that part of your portfolio in a bank, or even a taxable money market fund. Your choices turn mostly on what you do with the income—spend it or save it.

If you're spending your interest income as you earn it, consider these alternatives:

- U.S. Treasuries and Treasury money markets funds are free from state income tax.
- Municipal money market funds are free from federal and most state income taxes
- Immediate annuities pay a portion of your income in the form of tax-free return of principal.

If you're accumulating your interest income, consider these alternatives:

- Fixed annuities and variable annuity fixed accounts work much like a tax-deferred bank CD.
- A variable annuity money market fund is a money market fund in a tax-deferred wrapper. High contract charges may erase the advantage of tax deferral. However, there are several low-load or no-load variable annuities that offer tax deferral with lower contract charges.

It may seem like a waste of tax deferral to hold money markets in your retirement plan. But, as you'll see in Chapter Six, the key to making the most of tax deferral is to shelter your least efficient investments. If taxable money market funds make more sense than tax-free funds, then a retirement account may in fact be the place to hold your cash.

There's no problem moving out of money market funds because there's no capital gains tax to avoid. (There may be a penalty for moving certificates of deposit.) Simply choose a better tax-advantaged alternative and fire away.

Fixed Accounts and Stable Value Funds

If your employer's retirement plan is invested in a group variable annuity, or you've bought a variable annuity on your own, you probably have a "fixed account" investment option. If your employer's retirement plan is invested in mutual funds, you may also have a stable value fund. Don't overlook this option! Fixed accounts and stable value accounts can help you reduce portfolio risk and boost your return at the same time.

Many investors use cash and bonds solely to reduce risk, as measured by volatility. If cash and bonds "zig" while stocks "zag," the overall result is a less volatile portfolio. The cash and bonds "anchor" the stocks and reduce overall volatility. They aren't in your portfolio to improve perform-ance. How can they, when they return so much less over time?

Fixed accounts and stable value accounts give you the return of an intermediate-term bond, with the reduced volatility of cash. This makes them a more effective anchor than cash (because they pay more) or bonds (because of their lower volatility). And they actually let you invest more in stocks

The downside of the fixed account is liquidity. There's generally a limit on how much you can transfer out of the fixed account in any given year. (Stable value funds generally offer more liquidity, but pay slightly lower rates.) Still, if you're investing for the long run, these limits shouldn't cramp your style. And fixed accounts are backed by the assets of the insur-ance company that offers the fund. You'll need to do some homework to make sure it's a company you can trust.

2.2   U.S. Government Securities

The United States is the world's largest creditor. Ironically, it's also the world's *safest* creditor. Investment analysts use Treasury bills as their proxy for risk-free returns. Foreigners often buy Treasuries rather than invest in their own currencies. And when the Russian ruble collapses, or Asian economies get the flu, investors flee to the quality of Treasuries.

The U.S. government and its agencies issue a wide variety of bonds. Each of them has different tax twists, discussed below.

2.2.1   Treasuries

U.S. Treasuries are bonds issued by the U.S. Treasury and backed by the full faith and credit of the United States government. This is an even safer guarantee than FDIC insurance. If the FDIC defaults, it will be the Treasury bailing it out. And if the Treasury ever defaults, it won't matter where you put your money. (By that point, you'll wish you were living in a shack in Montana.) Treasuries include bills (maturities up to one year), notes (maturities between one and 10 years), and bonds (maturities over 10 years).

Treasury interest is free from state and local income taxes. Your taxable equivalent yield equals the Treasury rate divided by 100 minus your state rate. If your state tax rate is 10%, a Treasury paying 7.00% is equal to a fully taxable bond paying 7.78%. Obviously, there's no tax advantage to buying Treasuries in a state with no income tax.

Since Treasuries are so safe, the Treasury can pay less interest and still attract enough buyers to finance the government. If credit risk isn't an issue with you, the state and local tax savings may not be enough to offset the lower yield.

Treasuries are available from any bank or brokerage house. You can also buy them directly in denominations of $1,000 and up through the Treasury Direct program (202-874-4000, Option 5). If you have less than $50,000 to buy Treasuries, use a fund for proper diversification. Most treasury funds differ little from each other. If you buy funds, pay careful attention to average maturities, which determine price volatility, and expense ratios. These can add up over time and make a tremendous difference in your long-term total return.

Treasury bills, with maturities up to one year, don't pay periodic interest. Instead, they're issued at a discount to their face value at maturity. The difference between the discounted price you pay and the $1,000 you eventually receive is taxed as income at maturity. You don't owe tax until the year the T-bill matures. So if you bought a one-year T-bill on February 1, 1999, you could earn 11 months of interest, and pay no tax until you file your 2000 return in 2001.

2.2.2 Treasury Inflation Protection Securities

Treasury Inflation Protection Securities, or TIPS, are a new class of Treasury securities indexed to inflation. Each year, your interest and your face value rises (or falls!) with the consumer price index. The rising interest, naturally, is taxable as you receive it. The principal value resets each year to reflect the rise in the consumer price index. TIPS have proven popular since their introduction. But here's a potential problem: your rising principal is taxed as current income as well as your interest. (Your annual gain is taxed as original issue discount and reported to you on Form 1099-OID.) If inflation soars like it did in the 1970s, you could wind up paying hefty taxes on paper gains.

Let's say that in 1998, you pay $1,000 for a 10-year TIP. The bond pays a stated interest rate of 3%. The 1998 inflation rate is 4%. At the end of 1998, your bond's value will rise to $1,040, and your annual interest will increase to $31.20, or 3% of $1,040. You'll owe tax that year on the $30 interest and $40 inflation adjustment. Next year, you'll owe tax on the $31.20 interest, plus that year's inflation adjustment.

TIPS pay a lower stated interest rate in exchange for inflation protection. But since both the interest and principal gain are taxed as ordinary income each year, they're best suited for tax-advantaged accounts.

2.2.3 Agencies

U.S. agency securities are issued by U.S. governmental agencies. They usually consist of federally funded or guaranteed loans that are packaged and sold to investors. Agencies issuing securities include the Federal National Mortgage Agency, or "Fannie Mae" (mortgages) and the Student Loan Marketing Agency, or "Sallie Mae" (student loans). Agency securities aren't backed by the full faith and credit of the U.S. Treasury and aren't free from state and local taxes. They pay slightly higher interest to make up for these disadvantages.

Mortgage-backed securities have a tax twist of their own. Usually a portion of every payment is a tax-free return of your own principal. The concept is easy to grasp if you think of the bond as an actual mortgage. Every payment you make includes part of the principal. So if you're the bank, every monthly payment includes a portion of your original loan principal. The principal boosts your monthly payment. It makes your yield look awfully high in comparison to regular Treasury bonds. But remember, like a mortgage, there's nothing left at the end! If you spend all of your income without reserving your principal, you'll wind up broke at the end.

What's more, your payments will rise and fall as interest rates change. Let's say you buy a Ginnie Mae. If interest rates drop, homeowners will refinance their existing mortgages. If the homeowners in your pool of mortgage refinance, you'll get back large chunks of principal. What's worse, you'll have to reinvest at lower rates. Conversely, if rates rise, homeowners will hold on to their low-rate loans. You'll get back less to reinvest at the new, higher rates.

Collateralized mortgage obligations, or CMOs, are the ultimate form of these securities. The investment bank that puts together these securities divides each pool of mortgages into classes called "tranches" with differing claims to the income and principal. The first tranche might receive principal and interest payments for the first 12 months. This would be a relatively safe security, with little risk of sudden rate drops or economic uncertainty that would threaten expected payments. The last tranche might receive principal and interest payments, *if any*, from the last 12 months of the pool—20 or more years out! (These final tranches are nicknamed "toxic waste" to reflect their risk.) Wall Street professionals make millions packaging and trading CMOs with every twitch of the economy. But make sure you understand exactly what you're buying before you put down your money. And make sure you understand how much return to expect in the form of taxable interest and nontaxable principal.

This same principal applies with any asset-backed debt. Lenders such as General Motors Acceptance Corporation (GM's car loan arm) are securitizing pools of car loans and even credit card debt. (They're doing it because their investment bankers can make a buck doing it—not because you have any business buying them.)

2.2.4 Savings Bonds

U.S. Savings Bonds aren't as dull as they used to be. Their main appeal has been patriotism, not returns. But that has changed, and now savings bonds pay a market rate tied to Treasury yields. And they have attractive tax advantages. You can report your interest income every year *or* when you redeem the bond. Savings bond interest you use to pay for college costs may be tax-free depending on your income.

New Series EE and HH savings bonds are issued at half their face value. The bond's redemption value grows monthly or semiannually according to tables published annually. Bonds issued between May 1, 1995 and April 30, 1997, pay 85% of the average six-month T-bill rate for the first five years and 85% of the five-year Treasury rate for the next 12 years. New bonds issued after April 30, 1997, earn 90% of the average market yield on five-year Treasuries for the preceding six months. If the bonds haven't reached their face value in 17 years, the Treasury will reset the redemption value at that time.

New Series I inflation-indexed savings bonds are issued at face value and grow for up to 30 years. The Treasury declares an earnings rate for the six-month period during which you buy the bond. The Treasury also declares a semiannual inflation adjustment. You can redeem your bond any time after six months. However, if you redeem within the first five years after issue, you'll pay a penalty of three months' interest. You can buy up to $30,000 worth in a year. Here's how they help you with your taxes:

- You can include the annual gain on your tax return if you choose. Or you can include your accumulated gain the year you redeem the bond.
- You can change from annual reporting to deferral, and vice versa. To change from annual reporting to deferral, file *Form 3115* the year you stop reporting annual gain. You have to continue deferring at least five years following the year of the change. To change from deferral to annual reporting, simply report the accumulated gain that year and annual gain as you receive it in future years.
- Savings bond interest, like other federal interest, is free from state and local taxes.
- Series EE and Series I bonds you redeem to pay your children's college tuition may be partially or fully tax-free if your income is below $65,850 ($106,250 for joint filers; 1998 figures).
- If you buy a bond in a child's name and report the interest annually, the gain in the bond's value may be subject to the *kiddie tax.* If your kids report interest annually and the income grows to the point where they face the tax, change to deferral reporting until they reach 14 and the tax no longer applies.

2.3 Municipal Bonds

Municipal bonds, or munis, are issued by cities, counties, and their agencies, including universities, water and sewer districts, and municipally backed private activities such as stadiums and aquariums. General obligation bonds are backed by the issuer's entire receipts. Revenue bonds are backed by the revenue from a specific activity—a stadium, bridge, dam, or other project. Credit quality ranges from AAA-rated insured bonds all the way down to municipal junk. There are literally thousands of municipal bond issuers spread across the country.

Munis are called tax-free bonds because their interest income is free from federal income tax. These are a traditional favorite for high-income investors, and there are entire firms that do nothing but underwrite and trade municipal bonds. But they're not as simple as their name implies.

Since municipal bond interest is income tax-free, issuers can pay lower rates. The key rate is taxable equivalent yield—the rate you'd have to get with a taxable bond to equal the muni's tax-free yield. Your taxable equivalent yield equals the muni bond rate divided by (100 minus your tax rate). If you're in the 28% tax bracket, a muni paying 5.00% equals a taxable bond paying 6.94% (5.00 divided by .72). If you're in the 39.6% bracket, the same muni equals a taxable bond paying 8.28% (5.00 divided by .604).

Taxable Equivalent Yields									
Tax Rate	4%	5%	6%	7%	8%	9%	10%	11%	12%
15%	4.71	5.88	7.06	8.24	9.41	10.59	11.76	12.94	14.12
28%	5.56	6.94	8.33	9.72	11.11	12.50	13.89	15.28	16.67
31%	5.80	7.25	8.70	10.14	11.59	13.04	14.49	15.94	17.39
36%	6.25	7.81	9.38	10.94	12.50	14.06	15.63	17.19	18.75
39.6%	6.62	8.28	9.93	11.59	13.25	14.90	16.56	18.21	19.87

State and local taxes also affect your true taxable equivalent yield. If you're comparing a municipal bond's yield against a Treasury bond, include state tax only if your state taxes the muni bond interest. If you're comparing a municipal bond's yield against a fully taxable corporate or foreign bond, include all state and local taxes. If you're collecting Social Security, don't forget to include the effect of tax on Social Security benefits. In some cases, a muni bond makes more sense than a taxable bond, even when the taxable equivalent yield is lower, because the taxable bond subjects more of your Social Security benefit to tax. And municipal bonds are even more valuable if your income is high enough to phase out exemptions, deductions, and credits. Muni bond interest doesn't increase your AGI, so the true taxable equivalent yield is even higher.

In the 15% bracket, municipal bonds make no sense. Your after-tax yield will be higher with Treasuries or fully taxable bonds. In the 28% bracket, yields are more competitive. You should check each time you buy to see whether municipal after-tax equivalents beat taxable alternatives. And in the 31% bracket or above, municipals nearly always net more after taxes than any taxable bonds except junk. Tax-preparation software can help you or your tax advisor calculate which bonds will yield most in your particular case—municipals, Treasuries, or fully taxable corporates.

Municipal bonds' after-tax advantages typically rise as maturities increase and, in the case of funds, expenses fall. Muni money market and bond fund expenses swallow a larger percentage of gross yields than taxable funds—expenses remain constant even though municipal yields are lower. But longer-term bonds and bond funds with low expenses are likelier to pay off, especially in the 28% bracket. And if you're stretching for yield, don't ignore municipal junk. Many municipal bond issuers choose not to obtain ratings for small issues. These unrated issues are called municipal junk. Municipal junk can be an excellent choice for income investors.

Here are the specific tax rules for municipal bonds:

- Municipal bond interest income is free from regular federal income tax.
- Most municipal bonds are free from state tax in the state of issue.
- Puerto Rico bonds and funds are free from state tax in any state. These may be attractive to investors in states that tax their own bonds.
- Municipal bonds values are subject to federal estate tax.
- Private activity municipal bonds issued to finance stadiums and similar projects are subject to the alternative minimum tax.
- If you sell a municipal bond, your gain or loss is taxed as capital gain or loss.

- If you buy a municipal bond at a premium—a price above its face value—you'll have to amortize the premium over the remaining term of the bond. With muni bonds, amortization doesn't reduce the interest you receive. That's because you pay no tax on the interest to begin with. Amortization just reduces your basis for figuring gain or loss on the sale.

- Since gains and losses on sales are taxable, muni bonds make great candidates for tax swaps. If your bond's value falls, you can sell it to realize a capital loss. You can use the proceeds to buy a new bond and increase your income, improve your credit quality, and lengthen or shorten your bond's maturity, all at the same time.

- Zero-coupon municipal bonds pay no current interest. Instead, you buy the bond at a deep discount to face value. The value of the bond increases steadily as it moves towards maturity, finally maturing at face value. Since muni bond interest is not taxed, you pay no tax on the gain if you hold to maturity. All of your gain will be considered interest. But if you sell the bond before maturity, you'll have to calculate how much of your gain consists of nontaxable interest and how much consists of taxable capital gain. The process works the same as with any other zero-coupon bond.

- Never buy a municipal bond or fund in a tax-deferred account. Not only do you earn a lower rate; you convert tax-free interest into ordinary income. This might seem like an obvious mistake. But IRA custodians report hundreds of tax-deferred accounts holding municipal bonds and funds.

Municipal bond funds and unit investment trusts (closed-end, unmanaged muni bond portfolios packaged and sold by brokers) come in all shapes and sizes. Tax-free money market funds invest in short-term municipal bonds to maintain a stable net asset value and pay tax-free income. Short-term, intermediate-term, and long-term bond funds serve investors seeking specific maturities. Insured funds buy insured bonds for ultimate safety; while high-yield funds buy lower-rated and unrated municipal junk for highest yields. Finally, national funds buy bonds from all across America, while single-state funds invest in a single state to avoid state income tax in that state. Income dividends are tax-free; capital gains distributions and sales of fund shares are taxable.

If you have less than $500,000 to buy munis, you should buy mutual funds. Funds give you instant diversification among issuers and maturities. This can cut both your credit risk and interest rate risk. Funds will also reinvest your interest at the same rate as the rest of your money if you aren't spending the interest. (If you buy individual bonds, it's hard to reinvest the small semiannual interest payments.) Fund managers have the specialized expertise to evaluate credit quality and the clout to buy at the best price.

Single state funds are popular in states that don't tax their own bonds. The obvious advantage is double tax-free income: interest is free from both federal and state income taxes. New York City residents can buy New York City bond funds for triple tax-free income. That's no small victory in a city where total taxes can mug you for more than 50%. The less obvious disadvantage of single state funds is the loss of diversification: all your muni bond eggs are in a single state's basket. This can affect your bond's values if your state or region goes into recession. Single state funds are also more expensive than their national counterparts. Costs are spread over fewer shareholders. And in-state demand for local bonds—especially insured bonds—may push up prices. These extra expenses can eat up your state tax savings, particularly with money market funds. However, if you live in a high-tax state like California or New York, it may pay to find a single-state fund with low expenses.

Here's a curious investment: single-state funds for states with no income tax. Why on earth would you buy a single-state fund, with less diversification and higher fees, except to avoid state taxes? So why on earth would you buy such a fund for a state with no tax to avoid? This is a real marketing triumph, especially with higher expenses on single state funds.

2.4 Corporate Bonds

Private corporations issue bonds to finance operations and expansions. Maturities range from commercial paper (90 days or less) to 40 years, while credit quality ranges from AAA-rated utilities to speculative junk. A corporate bond's tax efficiency will vary with its coupon rate, its maturity, and its credit quality. Shorter-term and lower-credit bonds are generally less efficient than longer-term, lower-credit bonds.

2.4.1 Convertible Bonds

Convertibles bonds are corporate bonds that are convertible into stock at a specified price. They give you all the profit potential of common stock along with the security of regular interest payments. These interest payments are usually higher than a typical dividend. At the same time, convertibles have a fixed maturity date, limited liquidity

If you convert your bond into stock, there's no tax due until you sell the stock. Your basis in the stock will be the same as in the original bond, and your holding period will start with the date you bought the bond. Convertibles are good for cautious investors who want a chance to profit from stock moves but keep an interest-paying safety cushion. But the high coupon makes them less efficient than straight common stock. If you're not spending your interest income as you earn it, confine your convertibles to your tax-deferred accounts.

2.4.2 Junk Bonds

When you think of junk bonds, you might think of Michael Milken and the 1980s-style corporate raiders who used them to leverage their way into fortunes. But junk bonds (or, to those who underwrite and sell them, high-yield bonds) are simply bonds without an investment-grade rating. This may include bonds from small and mid-sized companies looking to finance growth, to fallen angels experiencing financial difficulty that costs them their investment-grade rating. (Municipal junk includes bonds from troubled issuers like New York City in the 1970s and Orange County in 1994 and bonds from issuers who don't want to pay the price for a rating. You can probably consider many foreign bonds, especially emerging markets bonds, to be junk as well.) What they all share are high current yields plus good potential for capital gains. Domestic corporate junk carries higher credit risk than investment-grade bonds. Maturities usually fall into the short-intermediate range, so interest-rate risk is low. As an asset subclass, it's an excellent choice for high total return with less volatility than stocks. Most individual investors buy their junk in the form of mutual funds—the market is just too specialized for amateurs.

Corporate junk is taxed the same as other corporate bonds. But since junk bonds pay the highest available interest, it naturally follows that they generate the highest tax bills as well. For this reason, junk bonds are best suited for tax-deferred retirement accounts and variable annuities. And junk bonds have another twist that makes them even less tax-efficient. In many cases, a junk bond fund's total return will be lower than the income dividend it pays. This is because a small percentage of the holdings will default, either missing payments or becoming worthless altogether. Junk's higher income compensates for this risk. But this has the effect of returning a portion of your original capital—the portion that defaults—in the form of taxable interest.

Finally, junk bond issuers (and other corporate issuers) sometimes pay bondholders "consent money" in order to consent to changes in the bond's indenture—the debt agreement that governs the terms of the bond. This consent money is taxable as ordinary income. If you invest through funds, there's no need to worry about this treatment. The fund simply pays through your proportional share.

2.4.3 Loan Participations

Loan participations are a special class of corporate debt—syndicated bank loans. A bank underwrites the loan, then splits it up into pieces, selling them to various buyers. This lets the lender collect the fee for underwriting and syndicating the loan without bearing all of the credit risk. There are several mutual funds that make this class of security available to retail investors. Usually they are closed-end funds or restrict withdrawals to certain specified periods, such as the last two weeks of each calendar quarter.

Loan participations are nearly always tied to the prime rate. Your interest income rises and falls with interest rate changes. This reduces price volatility and nearly eliminates interest-rate risk. This price stability makes loan participations a valuable hedge against rising interest rates. But it also means that nearly all of your gains will come in the form of current interest, taxable immediately at your highest rate. This inefficiency, along with limited liquidity, makes loan participation funds most appropriate for tax-deferred accounts.

2.5   Foreign Bonds

Foreign bonds are issued by governments and corporations outside the U.S. Many investment advisors avoid foreign bonds in the belief that their higher credit risk, volatility, and exposure to currency moves as well as interest-rate swings add up to too much risk for U.S. investors. If you buy foreign bonds, don't do it on your own. Find a good fund.

Foreign bonds follow the same general tax rules as U.S. bonds. The more credit risk and interest-rate risk you accept the more total return you'll be able to draw in the form of capital gain. But foreign bonds carry two special tax twists of their own:

- If your fund pays foreign income taxes on the income it earns, you have three ways to use them to cut your bill. You can deduct them with state and local taxes on Schedule A. You can take a credit for up to $300 in foreign taxes on Form 1040 ($600 for joint filers). Or you can take a credit on Form 1116.
- Many foreign bonds pay a higher nominal interest rate than comparable U.S. bonds. This may reflects high inflation in the issuing country. As time passes, the foreign country's currency depreciates against the dollar, bringing the foreign issuer's real interest rates back in line with ours. But in the meantime, you'll pay extra tax on the nominal income that actually consists of inflationary gain. This makes the higher tax on foreign bond interest even worse.

Bond Investing Strategies

There's more to choosing a bond than simply searching for the highest yield—or even the highest after-tax yield. The true measure of a bond is after-tax total return, which turns on credit quality and duration.

If you're spending your interest income as you earn it:

- If you're concerned with credit quality, choose U.S. Treasuries to avoid state and local income taxes.
- Municipal bond and bond fund interest income is free from most federal and state income taxes.
- Immediate annuities return a portion of your income in the form of tax-free return of principal.

If you're reinvesting your interest income for further gains:

- You can compound municipal bond and bond fund income over time.
- If you're in the 15% tax bracket, hold your bonds in tax-deferred retirement accounts.
- Variable annuity fixed income subaccounts work like mutual funds with a tax-deferred wrapper.
- Whole life, universal life, and variable life insurance fixed-income subaccounts offer tax-deferred growth for buyers who need life insurance protection.

Switching to a more tax-efficient bond portfolio shouldn't be too painful. If you own bond funds with large reinvested gains, remember that those reinvested dividends add to your basis and won't increase your tax. If you own bonds or funds with paper losses, consider selling now and realizing those losses before buying tax-advantaged alternatives such as immediate annuities. If you own bonds or funds that would produce a taxable capital gain, consider whether today's tax justifies tomorrow's savings.

Investing for Income

Most income investors look to bonds first for the relatively high interest income. But it's a mistake to invest solely for income and ignore future growth. Fixed-income investments generally pay a lower total return in exchange for the safety of the income stream. So if you invest solely for income, you give up potential growth. Also, investing for income means earning the bulk of your return in the form of interest income, taxable today at your highest rate. If you invest for growth, you can draw your income from long-term capital gains, taxed when you sell at lower rates. This gives you the best of both worlds—higher income and lower taxes. The price, of course, is higher volatility than with fixed-income-only investments.

Investing for income also leaves you dangerously exposed to inflation. You already know that inflation eats away at your purchasing power. If you buy a $100,000 Treasury paying 7%, and inflation runs 3%, at the end 30 years your $7,000 income will be worth just $4,116. But inflation makes your tax bite worse by converting part of your principal into taxable income. At the end of 30 years, your principal will be worth just $58,800 of today's dollars. And you'll be paying tax on income equal to 11.9% of that principal, rather than your original 7%. So inflation makes your tax bite worse by converting principal into taxable income.

The solution is to invest for high total return consisting of income and capital growth. The capital growth protects your principal and your income from inflation. And it lets you take a part of your income in the form of long-term capital gains, taxed when you sell at lower rates.

Chapter 3

Equities

As we discussed in Chapter One, there are really just two ways to invest your money: loan or own. Chapter Two covered "loaning" your money, in the form of cash and bonds. This Chapter covers "owning." Stocks are the main equity asset class, and the one we think of first when we think of equity. But there are plenty of other equity classes, including real estate, commodities, collectibles, and classic tax shelters such as oil and gas and equipment leasing. Equities also include "derivatives"—securities whose prices are "derived" from some underlying equity, such as options and futures.

Ownership is fundamentally more tax-efficient. You can pay your tax when you choose to sell. And, if you hold your investment for more than 12 months, you can pay lower long-term gain rates. But capital gains are just the first place to look for lower taxes. This Chapter tells you how to choose the most efficient equities for your needs. You'll also learn how to buy and sell them as efficiently as possible. Finally, you'll learn some strategies to draw profits from your investments without selling at all.

3.1   Stock Investing Styles

Stocks represent ownership of a company. When you buy stock, you're actually buying a piece of the company, one that entitles you to elect a board of directors, vote on various corporate issues, and receive dividends the board might choose to pay. As the company's earnings grow, the company's value grows, and your piece of the business grows more valuable. As the share price rises, so do your profits. At least, that's how it's *supposed* to work.

Stocks pay you now, with income dividends, and later, with capital gains. Cash dividends are taxed as ordinary income in the year the company pays the dividend. Profit or loss is treated as capital gain or loss when you sell. Since most stocks return more in capital gains than they do in income, stocks are considered tax-advantaged. This is far more valuable now, with dividend yields at historical lows, than it was in previous years when dividend yields were higher and there was less difference between ordinary-income and capital-gain rates.

3.1.1 Growth and Value

You probably already know that different stock investment styles give you different results. Small, growth stocks can rocket up and down with the day's headlines, while stodgier utility stocks give smoother, more predictable returns. However, your investment style affects your tax bill, too. The main culprit is dividend income. Dividends are taxed as ordinary income, now, at your highest rate, while appreciation is taxed as capital gain, when you sell, at potentially lower rates. And different investment styles—specifically, "value" and "growth"—are characterized by differing reliance on dividends.

There's no single accepted definition of value—like beauty, it's in the eye of the beholder. Value investors typically look for stocks they consider undervalued relative to some objective measure such as earnings (measured by the price/earnings ratio), dividends (the dividend yield), sales (the price/sales ratio), or book value (the book-to-market ratio). They also look for stocks that have been beaten down by temporary circumstances, like Exxon after the *Exxon Valdez* spill, Union Carbide after the

Bhopal disaster, or anyone else after they announce they're going to miss their earnings forecast. Their goal is to buy low and profit when prices rebound. Value stocks are often mature companies paying higher dividends than growth stocks. These dividends help cushion share prices from further declines and smooth out market swings. They can drag down tax efficiency by throwing off currently taxable income. But there's no shortage of "value" stocks with low price/earnings, price/sales, and price/book value ratios that don't pay a dividend.

Growth investors, in contrast, look for fast-growing companies expected to produce above-average earnings to drive share prices higher. They don't mind buying high if they think they can sell even higher. Growth stocks usually pay little or no dividend, choosing instead to plow profits back into the company. These lower dividends make growth stocks as a group more tax-efficient than value stocks. Growth stocks are also generally more volatile, because there's no dividend to cushion price swings. This works to your advantage—*if* you can tolerate the volatility—because you can use your losers to offset ordinary income and capital gains. But volatility has its obvious downside. Tax losses are losses! If you can't stand the thought of quick losses, find another way to hold down tax on your investments.

The naive investor might think that growth stocks are better because they pay lower dividends. But remember, your real goal isn't just low taxes—it's high after-tax returns. Several academic studies show that value stocks outperform growth stocks over time. This may make value stocks a better choice even in the face of higher dividends.

Morningstar Mutual Funds rates funds and fund categories, among other yardsticks, by percent pre-tax return, a measure of tax efficiency that adjusts pre-tax returns for taxes due on income and capital gains distributions. Funds aren't perfect proxies for their underlying styles. They carry management fees and administrative expenses that eat into returns, and trading boosts realized capital gains. But, Morningstar reports that small-cap funds are more tax-efficient than large-cap funds, and growth funds more efficient than value funds.

3.1.2. Sector Selection

Stock market sectors are broad industry classes, such as technology, natural resources, financials, consumers, and health care. Research suggests that sector selection is even more powerful than market timing. One study, conducted by CDA/Weisenberger, looked at growth of $1,000 for three strategies for the period January 1, 1981 through October 31, 1997:

- A "buy and hold" portfolio simply tracked the S&P 500 for the entire period. This portfolio returned $12,982, or 16.45% per year.
- A market timing portfolio moved in and out of cash and the S&P 500 with perfect foresight in predicting all market swings lasting three months or longer. This portfolio returned $45,113, or 25.39% per year.
- Finally, a sector rotation strategy moved into each year's top-performing sector, shifting each December 31 with perfect foresight into the next year's top-performing sector. This portfolio returned a whopping $117,975, or 32.76% per year.

The problem, of course, is that these numbers assume these portfolios pay no taxes. Although the CDA/Weisenberger study didn't calculate after-tax values, you can be sure that buying and holding looks more attractive after subtracting out taxes.

It makes sense that different market sectors perform differently over time. That's because changing economic circumstances affect industries differently. It's important to realize that market sectors have different tax consequences too. Some sectors—notably technology—throw off few, if any, taxable dividends. These sectors are the most tax-efficient. Other sectors, such as utilities and real estate investment trusts, throw off higher taxable dividends for less efficient performance. Be sure you understand the different tax consequences of your chosen sectors.

Remember, the proper goal is to earn the highest after-tax return, consistent with your own willingness to take risk. That's important—in fact, it might be more important than actual return. If you lie awake at night in fear of a market crash, you won't do yourself any favors buying Internet start-ups to avoid tax on dividends.

3.1.3 The Dogs of the Dow

The "dogs Of The Dow^{sm}" is a popular, proven strategy for beating the Dow Jones Industrial Average. The theory is simple: stocks with high dividends outperform the average as a whole. Yields are high, the theory says, because prices have fallen too low. These low prices set the stage for a comeback. The high dividend boosts your return even further. The actual mechanics are simple: each year, rank the 30 stocks comprising the Dow Jones Industrial Average according to dividend yield. Buy equal dollar amounts of the 10 stocks with the highest dividend yield. Hold the stocks for a year, and repeat the process annually. More aggressive investors buy the five lowest-priced stocks from among the 10 highest dividend yields. And the *Motley Fool* web site recommends a four-company version of the strategy they dub the "foolish four." If you can't afford to buy individual stocks, you can buy mutual funds, unit investment trusts (UITs), and variable annuity subaccounts that use the "dogs" strategy.

Results have been impressive. From 1972 to 1989, the dogs returned 19.03%, compared to 12.66% for the Dow and 12.79% for the S&P 500. Since 1989, the "dogs" have beaten the Dow just 4 times. Some critics argue that as the strategy has become popular, the market inefficiency it exploits has disappeared. However, I suspect this is due to the general underperformance by value stocks, and not any failure of the strategy.

Impressive as they are, can you see how these dogs practically sit up and beg the IRS to grab your gains? The high dividend yields are taxed as ordinary income immediately. And the constant annual turnover clips your profits every time you sell. You can hold your stocks for a year and a day to take advantage of lower long-term capital gain rates. But you still whack your profits with each substitution—generally, two to five each year. After taxes, the "dogs" lag a plain-vanilla S&P 500 index fund. The popular Dow "Target 10" UITs sold by Merrill Lynch, Paine Webber, Prudential, and other Wall Street firms are even deadlier because they sell each stock at the expiration of the trust. This forces you to pay tax on all of your winners, not just those that drop out of the top 10. So kennel these dogs in your tax-deferred accounts.

3.1.4 Preferred Stock

Preferred stock pays a guaranteed dividend that has to be paid before common shareholders get any dividend. If the company goes bankrupt, preferred shareholders get a preferred crack at what's left of the wreckage. The higher dividend makes the stock itself trade more like a bond. Convertible preferred is preferred stock that can be converted into common stock at a specified price. These shares pay a lower dividend than regular preferred in exchange for the conversion privilege.

Preferred stock doesn't just *trade* more like a bond—it's *taxed* like a bond. Paying today's tax on today's dividend takes away much of the tax advantage of buying stock. Tax-efficient investors don't buy preferred stock. That's why this book spends just 124 words on the subject.

3.2 Stock Investing Strategies

Now that we've discussed the tax effects of stock investing styles, let's look at some strategies to sort out which help you fight the tax man.

3.2.1 Minimize Turnover

"Investors are overconfident. Overconfidence leads to too much trading. And trading is hazardous to your wealth." These are the conclusions of Brad M. Barber and Terrance Odean, professors at the Graduate School of Management, University of California, Davis. Their study, *Trading is Hazardous to Your Wealth*, surveyed 66,465 investors with accounts at a large discount brokerage. During the study period, from 1991 through 1996, the market returned 17.9%. The average investor earned 16.4%. Investors who traded the most earned just 11.4%.

The stock market crashes every time you sell a winner. Why? Because the taxes you pay on your profits take a bite out of every gain. If you trade stocks like a politician tells lies, you'll whack your gains even harder than if you buy and hold. Not only do you whack your gain more often, but every dollar of tax you pay costs you the chance to make that dollar grow. For this reason, you should be extra careful before you sell a stock

Just how much harder does turnover make it to reach your investment goals? Let's assume that you have $100,000 in a taxable account, and you'd like to grow it to $200,000 in five years. That's an ambitious goal under any circumstances—but how much harder will it be with the tax man on your back? If you trade frequently, so that all of your gains are taxed at a regular 28% rate, you'll have to earn a whopping 20.65% per year to reach your $200,000 goal. If you hold your positions longer, so that all gains are taxed each year at just 20%, you'll need to earn just 18.59%. That's a considerable improvement. But if you buy and hold your entire portfolio for the entire five years, so that you generate no taxes during that period, you'll need to earn just 14.87% to produce a $100,000 gain.

"Aha!" you say. "If I trade every year, I'll have a $200,000 portfolio with no built-in tax liability. If I buy and hold, I'll have a $200,000 portfolio with a $100,000 built-in capital gain. I'll really have just $180,000 after paying tax on my capital gain!" That's true. So what will it take to generate a $225,000 portfolio—enough to pay the 20% tax on capital gain and still leave $200,000? The answer is, it will take 17.61%—still far less than the 20.65% you would need to earn if you pay tax on each year's gains at ordinary rates.

There's no shortage of research showing that frequent trading hurts your return. Experts in behavioral finance—a new academic discipline that studies how real-world investors act and react to real-world conditions—have conducted study after study to prove this point. For more information, see the "Introduction to Behavioral Finance" report available at the *undiscoveredmanagers* website.

The conclusion is simple and inescapable. Keep your trigger finger off your trading button. We'll cover this ground again and again as we discuss various strategies.

The one exception to the turnover rule is this: don't be afraid to walk away from a loser. The same experts in behavioral finance who tell us we trade too much also tell us that we hate losses almost three times as much as we enjoy gains. Faced with the choice between selling a winner and selling a loser, most of us sell the winner. That way, we don't have to admit we were wrong when we picked the loser. But dumping the winner costs you tax, and cuts your profits short. Selling the loser cuts your tax, and lets you reinvest in a winner. (One entertaining guidebook for new stockbrokers tells them how to get their clients to sell losing positions. Never tell them to take a loss, the book advises. Instead, tell them to "transfer your assets.")

3.2.2 Year-end Tax Selling

The "January effect" is a well-known theory that holds that stock prices—particularly small stocks—will rise in late December and, particularly, during the first five trading days of the new year. The reason, of course, is that investors are selling their losers to harvest the tax losses, and, in the process, pushing prices down. The result, literally, is stock on sale.

If you're going to play "the January game," here are two tips for coming out ahead. First, look for the companies that have experienced the biggest price drops. More sellers will look to these issues first, pushing prices down even farther. These are the stocks you'll want to buy. And second, don't wait until Christmas to sell your losers. By then, the sale will be on, and you'll get less for them than if you had already sold.

3.2.3 Identify Specific Shares to Sell

If you're like most investors, you've bought different lots of the same stock at different times and prices. This is especially true if you've bought shares through a dividend reinvestment program. You can control the tax you pay just by identifying shares to sell. If you hold certificates yourself, choose the highest-priced lot to pay the lowest tax. Or, if you have losers to match, choose the lowest-priced lot to realize the biggest gain without paying tax. If you hold shares in street name with a broker, simply instruct your broker to sell the highest-cost shares first. If you don't, the IRS will treat you as having sold your oldest shares first.

3.2.4 Match Gains and Losses

Matching gains and losses, so that your losses cancel out your gains, is a basic strategy for holding down tax when you do sell. Even if you have to sell, and report income now, you can eliminate tax by matching gains with offsetting losses. It makes sense to hold your losers until you can use them to wipe out a gain.

Let's take a closer look to see how you can use this strategy. Let's say you have two stocks worth $100. One has a built-in capital gain of $10; the other has a gain of $50. Which stock should you sell? The answer, of course, is the first. If you sell it for $100 and pay a 20% tax on your $10 gain, you'll have $98. If you invest it in a new stock that appreciates by 10%, you'll wind up with $107.80. Your 10% gain nets you just 7.8% after paying tax on the first stock's gain.

Do you have a fourth stock somewhere in your portfolio that you can sell at a loss? Is the tax saving more than the cost of selling the stock? If so, sell that stock at the same time you sell your winner. The loss may shelter your gain and offset the tax you owe on your winner.

Many investors wait until the end of the year to sell their losers. This may not always be the best timing. The artificial pressure on prices pushes down values for stocks that have declined during the year, while pushing up prices for more desirable replacements. This "January effect" is more pronounced with small stocks, which are generally more volatile. The solution here is to sell your losers before the year-end rush.

Of course, if you do your homework, you may not be able to use this strategy. One of my tax clients also does business with my own broker. We've matched winners and losers each time we've sold a position—and now, after this greatest bull market ever, she has no losers left.

3.2.5 Dividends to Capital Gains

Cash dividends are taxed immediately as ordinary income. There's no tax break on dividends like there is for long-term capital gains. However, you can time your stock sales to capture your final dividend as a long-term capital gain, taxable at lower rates. Stocks that pay dividends do so to investors who own them as of a certain date, called the record date. After the record date, the stock trades ex-dividend, meaning without the dividend. Naturally, the stock's price drops on that date by an amount roughly equal to the missing dividend. If you sell your stock just before it goes ex-dividend, when it's fat with the dividend amount, you get the full value of the stock *and* the dividend. However, you'll pay lower long-term capital gains rates on the dividend since you receive it as part of the sale price rather than a dividend payment. This strategy also works for mutual funds.

3.2.6 Short Sales

When you sell "short," you borrow shares of stock, sell them, and hope the stock's price goes *down*. Then you can buy it back to replace it at the lower price and profit from the fall. When it works, it's simply buying low and selling high—in reverse. Your closing date for figuring gain or loss is the date you deliver the replacement shares. While you hold a short position, you'll have to pay your broker the dividends paid on the stock. You can add your dividend to your basis, or, if you hold the short position 46 days or more, you can deduct it as investment interest. (See **Endnote** 2, "Write Off Investment Interest," for the rules.)

"Shorting against the box" is a strategy for deferring tax on stock sales until the next taxable year. When you short against the box, you sell borrowed shares of a stock that you already own. This lets you profit from your existing position (by selling an equal amount of shares) without paying tax like you would on a sale. At the same time, you hedge the value of your shares. If the price falls, the profit you make on the short position offsets the loss you take on your own shares.

Before the Taxpayer Relief Act of 1997, you could hold a short period forever without paying tax on the sale. Now, you can use this strategy to delay taxes only if you close your short position by January 30 of the following year *and* hold the underlying stock for 60 days more. You'll have to accept the risk that your stock's value can fall during that 60-day period. So, shorting against the box is not as useful as before. However, it's still worth considering to delay this year's tax bill until next year.

3.2.7　Dividend Reinvestment Plans

Dividend reinvestment plans (DRIPs) automatically reinvest your cash dividends into more stock. The original appeal was the chance to reinvest small amounts with no commission. And some companies even sell shares at a discount. But watch out! Each reinvestment is a separate transaction, with a separate cost basis and holding period. Most companies charge an annual fee that can add up to more than the load you would pay to buy a diversified mutual fund, or even more than the commissions you would pay to buy your shares from a broker. And not all companies offer DRIPs. Don't limit your universe of stock candidates to those that offer DRIPs.

If the plan gives you a discount on new shares, the discount is taxable as short-term gain when you buy the discounted shares.

3.2.8 Dividends Received in Stock

Stock dividends that you receive in the form of more stock generally aren't taxed when you receive them. Instead, they're taxed as capital gains when you sell the dividend shares. Your basis for determining gain or loss is your original cost in the stock, divided by your total number of shares. Your holding period for determining a short- or long-term gain is the date you bought the original stock. Tracking stocks—spin-off corporations that remain part of the parent for corporate income-tax purposes, such as the General Motors Class E shares that eventually became Electronic Data Systems—are also tax-free when distributed.

Let's say on January 1, 1997, you bought 100 shares of Microsplat for $1,100. On December 31, the company pays a dividend of 10 more shares. On August 1, 1998, you sell the dividend shares for $20 each. Your basis in the new shares is $10 each, which equals your $1,100 purchase price divided by 110 total shares. Your gain on the shares is $10 each, taxed as a long-term capital gain.

These stock dividends are taxed when they're paid:

- Preferred stock dividends
- Dividends paid in the stock of another company—say, shares in a subsidiary or sibling company in a controlled group

If you have a choice between taking cash or taking stock, the dividend is taxable when paid. Your holding period in the new shares begins the day after the distribution; your basis for figuring gain or loss is the value of the distribution.

If you reinvest your cash dividends in a dividend reinvestment program, the dividend is taxable when paid. If the plan lets you buy shares at a discount, your taxable basis for figuring gain or loss when you sell the new shares is the fair market value of the dividend date. There's no immediate tax on the discount—it's taxed as capital gain when you sell.

3.2.9 Portfolio Rebalancing

Once you've decided how much of your portfolio to allocate to stocks, bonds, cash, and other asset classes, market forces will affect each class differently. You might choose to put 50% in stocks, 40% in bonds, and 10% in cash. But at the end of the year, you might find that you have 52% in stocks, 39% in bonds, and just 9% in cash. And after five years, you might find yourself with 60% in stocks, 35% in bonds, and just 5% in cash. This new portfolio will behave differently than your original 50/40/10 mix.

Portfolio rebalancing is the process of moving money to restore your original allocation. Strictly speaking, it's not a stock investing strategy. It's an asset allocation tool. But most investors who rebalance their portfolios do it by selling stocks and reinvesting the proceeds into cash and bonds. So this is an appropriate place to discuss it. Some investors rebalance after a certain period of time—for example, quarterly or annually. Others rebalance only after the portfolio mix drifts by a certain percentage—for example, 7% for major asset classes such as stocks and bonds, and 5% for asset styles such as large-cap stocks and small-cap stocks. Portfolio rebalancing helps control risk, as measured by standard deviation of returns. It can also help improve your return by forcing you to take gains from recent winners and reallocate them to losers that might be poised to rebound.

The problem, of course, is that rebalancing requires you to sell appreciated assets and pay taxes. These taxes erase most of the gains from rebalancing. There are two solutions to the problem. The first is to confine rebalancing to your tax-deferred accounts. The second is to use new money, such as new contributions, interest, and dividends, to shore up your lagging asset classes. I recommend rebalancing only after market movement pushes an asset class beyond a specified percentage above or below your target. For example, you might ease up on stocks when market gains push your stock allocation more than 7% above your target. This lets you take advantage of rallies in a particular sector and gives you more control than a purely mechanical calendar period.

3.2.10 Day Trading

A mistake. For every Gen-X whiz kid making headlines and millions online, you'll find four washed-out failures slinking back to their day jobs with their tails between their legs. That's because 80% of day traders wind up *losing* money. You just don't hear about them. Except when they shoot up a brokerage in mid-town Atlanta.

Day trading is all about raw returns. There are no tax-efficient day trading strategies. But there are a few tricks to consider if you choose to take the plunge—or, more sensibly, if you choose to put part of your portfolio in a "fun money" trading account:

- You can trade inside your IRA so that you don't have to report gains and losses as you generate them. Instead, simply pay tax on your withdrawals.
- You can try to qualify as a professional trader. This will let you deduct all of your investment expenses, not just those that exceed 2% of your adjusted gross income. (See Endnote 1, "Write Off Investment Expenses," for more information.) But this is extremely difficult, and plenty of traders who've tried have gotten spanked. You'll need to show that
- If writing off investment expenses is your main concern, you can form a partnership or corporation to hold your accounout the usual 2% floor for individuals, then pass along the net profits. For example, you could

form a family limited partnership to hold the assets, then use an "S" corporation (one that pays no income tax on its own) to manage the partnership.

How to Pick Stocks

Picking stocks isn't rocket science. We've all seen stories about the little old lady down the street, or perhaps the retired couple next door, who amassed a fortune out of pennies and left it to a grateful local charity. If they can do it, so can you.

Here's an easy method for picking stocks that doesn't take a lot of time, effort, or money. Head to your local library and pick up a copy of the *Value Line Investment Survey*. Look for stocks rated "1" for value and "1" for timeliness. For the 35-year period ending June 1999, this group returned an astonishing 16,087%—far better than the Dow's 1,103% gain over the same period. Choose a stock from an industry that isn't already overrepresented in your portfolio that pays little or no dividend. Sit back and hold on.

Tuning Up Your Portfolio

It's not hard for a new investor to build a tax-efficient stock portfolio. It's harder for an experienced investor to tune up an existing portfolio. You can't turn a battleship on a dime, and you usually can't reallocate an existing portfolio without paying taxes on existing capital gains. You may net more, after taxes, with today's inefficient investments than you could net tomorrow after paying the capital gains taxes necessary to swap into existing investments. So, don't try to do it all at once.

The one exception to this rule involves inheritances. If you inherit an existing stock position or portfolio, you'll never have a better chance to make a change. *You* get the benefit of stepped-up basis, and you can sell without incurring the long-term capital gains tax your generous benefactor would have faced. Grandpa may have bought stock in the local phone company for forty years. His dying words may have been "never sell!" But, God love him, he's dead. It's your money now. If his stocks don't meet *your* needs for income, safety, and diversification, sell now, before it's too late. Save Grandpa's watch for sentiment. Put his stocks to work for yourself.

A Few Words on Beating the Market

We all want to beat the market. If you don't think you can do it yourselves, choose someone who can do it for us. The next Peter Lynch could be just a magazine cover away. And managing your money can be entertaining—something you do to pass the time and impress your friends and colleagues. But every time you trade, you play high-stakes poker with the world's best players—the mutual fund, pension, and endowment managers that dominate the market. Can you really beat the pros at their own game?

The disappointing reality is that the rewards of trying to beat the market don't justify the costs, particularly after taxes. Markets are too efficient, and managers are too skilled. Investment management has become a loser's game, where winners succeed by avoiding mistakes. The key to success isn't finding the next Microsoft. It's avoiding the next Boston Chicken.

Certainly, some managers succeed. However, beating the average—and even beating the market—is just as likely to result from luck as from skill.

Imagine we have 1,000 mutual fund managers all aiming to beat the average mutual fund return. At the end of their first year, 500 will succeed, with above average results. At the end of the second year, 250 of the first year's winners will beat the second year's average as well. At the end of the third year, 125 of the two-time winners will beat the third year's average. At this point, their funds' marketing departments will gear up to promote their records; their publicity departments will be arranging appearances. By the end of the sixth year, there will be 15 brilliant managers who have beaten the average *six years straight*. You'll see their faces on the cover of *Money*, and hear their opinions on CNBC. Yet, we can expect the same fantastic results from sheer luck.

The solution, for most investors and most markets, is indexing—buying mutual funds that hold a representative or complete sample of securities in order to track the appropriate benchmark. Index funds are cheap, reliable, effective ways to invest across asset classes. They free you from the burden of picking securities. They let you get on with the rest of your life. And they're wonderfully tax-efficient. So use index funds for your taxable funds and core asset classes—large-cap stocks, U.S. fixed income, and European and developed Asian markets. If you must take on the markets, save active management for tax-deferred accounts and less efficient markets, such as small stocks, emerging markets, and junk bonds that offer more chance for real profit.

There's no shortage of popular and academic guides that make a convincing case *against* active management. I especially recommend *Winning the Loser's Game: Timeless Strategies for Successful Investing* (McGraw-Hill, 3rd ed. 1998), a short but powerful argument against active management. Author Charles Ellis is a Wall Street legend and an entertaining writer who argues that the key to investment success is making fewer mistakes than your rivals.

3.3 Real Estate

Real estate is the foundation of more American fortunes than any other single investment. Even in today's high-tech economy, 27 members of the 1998 *Forbes 400* list of the richest Americans earned their fortune from real estate. It's the classic inflation hedge because it provides a steadily rising income. Each property is unique, with its own location, amenities, and tenant mix, so there's more opportunity to profit from market inefficiencies than with publicly traded securities. And real estate offers a special bonus for skittish investors uncomfortable with market volatility. It isn't marked to market at the end of each day like stocks and mutual funds. Your property's value rises and falls—but there's no daily price to ruin your morning coffee.

Income-producing rental properties include multifamily housing, commercial, and industrial property. (Raw land certainly qualifies as an investment. But it doesn't generate income and it's not depreciable. Buy it and hope the highway heads your way.) Investment real estate pays you now, with rent, and later, with long-term capital gain. But real estate qualifies for special tax breaks that shelter rental income. And it qualifies for more breaks to shelter your gain when you sell. Congress ended the glory days of real estate with the 1986 tax reform. The passive loss and at-risk rules ended abusive tax shelters, and real estate spiraled into a recession from which it's still recovering. However, real estate still offers tremendous opportunities for smart investors willing to do their homework. And real estate remains the nation's most tax-favored investment. These breaks include leverage, depreciation, tax-deferred growth, tax-free exchanges, and tax-deferred installment sales.

At the same time, real estate has some significant disadvantages relative to securities:

- Real estate is illiquid. You can't simply sell a property and close in three days the way you can with securities. There's no guarantee that you can sell your property when you want, for the price you want. And you'll probably have to pay a broker's hefty commission.
- Real estate is subject to complicated passive loss rules imposed to keep you from using passive losses to offset nonpassive income. Passive income is income from any trade or business in which you don't materially participate. You're considered to materially participate if you're involved in operations on a regular, continuous and substantial basis. This usually means performing substantially all the work of an activity or contributing more than 500 hours per year. However, rental real estate is considered a passive activity, so rental income and losses are passive income and losses. You can deduct passive losses against nonpassive income only if you qualify for the rental real estate loss allowance.
- Real estate is also subject to at-risk rules imposed to prevent you from writing off more than your actual investment. Amounts at risk are amounts that you can actually lose in an investment: cash contributions, your cost basis in property contributions, and loans for which you're personally on the hook. You can deduct as much in expenses as you have income to offset. Beyond that, you can only deduct as much as you actually have at risk in the investment. You can carry forward losses disallowed by the at-risk rule to offset future income.

3.3.1 Real Estate Tax Advantages

Let's look at some of real estate's tax advantages:

Leverage

Leverage is simply using borrowed money to buy your investment. Leverage lets you buy more property than you could afford on your own. This boosts your equity growth and depreciation deductions. If you choose your property carefully, the extra rent you earn should cover the mortgage. Let's say you put $20,000 down and finance $80,000 to buy a $100,000 four-family. In the next years, your property may appreciate $4,000, or 4%. While that may not sound like much, your equity in the property grows to $24,000—a full 20% gain. That's impressive in any investor's book.

You can use leverage to multiply your gains in other investments. If you put 20% down to buy stocks and your portfolio earns just 8%, you'll see your actual equity grow by a fantastic 40%. But you can borrow more of your purchase price with real estate (up to 100%) than you can with stocks (no more than 50%). And if the value of your real estate falls, there's no margin call as there would be with stocks. These advantages make leverage a more practical tool for real estate than for stocks.

Depreciation

Depreciation is writing off the cost of property over a specified life or recovery period. Depreciation shelters your income by giving you a paper tax loss without a corresponding cash flow reduction. You can write off a portion of your investment every year until you've written off nearly every dime. (There's no depreciation for raw land, and none for the land portion of any real estate investment.) Residential real estate depreciates over 27.5 years. Nonresidential real estate placed in service after May 12, 1993, depreciates over 39 years.

Let's say that you buy a four-family apartment for $180,000. $110,000 of the price is for the building and $70,000 is for the land. The building nets $4,000 after mortgage interest, utilities, and maintenance. However, you can depreciate $4,000 per year ($110,000 ⸱ 27.5). Your taxable income from the property is zero, and you pocket the $4,000 tax-free.

Depreciation reduces your basis in the property when you sell. There is a special 25% capital gains rate for recapture of depreciated deductions. Let's assume that in the example above, you had depreciated the property for four years, then sold the building for $200,000. Your gain on the sale would be $32,000. $12,000 is taxed as depreciation recapture at 25%. The rest is taxed as long-term capital gain at your regular long-term gain rate.

However, mortgage amortization, your actual principal payments, isn't deductible, even though it cuts your cash flow. If your mortgage amortization is more than your depreciation, the difference may be taxable income even though you don't receive any cash. This phantom income counts as passive income for purposes of the passive loss rule. So, passive losses (see below) can shelter your phantom income.

For example, you buy an apartment building in January 1998, for $100,000. You put $20,000 down and take out a 15-year mortgage at 8%. Your monthly mortgage payment is $764.25, and in the first year you pay $2,878.26 towards principal. Just 60% of your purchase price is depreciable, for a first-year depreciation deduction of $2,091. At the end of the year, your net cash flow leaves you with a $100 gain. Your depreciation deduction turns that into a net loss of $1,991. But wait! The $2,878.26 of your mortgage payment that goes towards principal isn't deductible. Your actual income on the property is $2,978.26—your $100 gain plus your $2,878.28 principal payment. Even after depreciation, you're left with $887.26 in taxable income, even though your cash flow nets you just $100.

Tax-Deferred Growth

Like any equity asset, your real estate equity grows tax-deferred. You pay no tax on your gain until you sell. When you do sell, you pay a lower long-term capital gains rate depending on when you bought it, how long you held it, and your regular tax bracket. (There's a special 25% tax to recapture amounts previously depreciated.) And if you die while you own the property, its value is stepped-up for your heirs.

Tax-free Exchanges

Internal Revenue Code Section 1031 lets you exchange one investment property for another "like-kind" investment property, tax-free. Like-kind property is liberally defined according to how you use the property—investment property, property held for business use, or residential property—and not character. You can exchange raw land for developed acreage, a city apartment for a suburban strip center, and even fee-simple property (outright ownership) for a leasehold of 30 years or longer. (You can't trade American property for foreign property.) Postponing the tax gives you the same advantage as an interest-free loan in the amount of tax you save. Here are the rules for 1031 exchanges:

- You have to hold both the old and new properties for investment. For example, you can't trade investment property for a primary residence.
- Both transfers have to happen within a 180-day period. If you don't specifically identify one of the properties to be traded, you have to do so within 45 days of the first transfer.
- If you receive additional property in the exchange—cash or nonlike-kind property—called "boot," you'll owe tax on the value of the boot.
- If you trade mortgaged property, the value of the mortgage released is boot. If both parties transfer mortgaged property, the one giving up the larger mortgage reports the difference in mortgage amounts as taxable boot.
- Ordinarily you can't declare a loss on a like-kind exchange. However, if you give up boot in the trade, you can declare the amount you give up as a loss.

- You have to carry over your basis in the old property to the new property. This limits the amount you can depreciate the new property.

You don't have to scour the classifieds to find property to trade yourself. You can find professional middlemen, called "exchange accomodators," within exchange firms, title companies, and law firms throughout the country. These exchange accomodators will make the necessary arrangements to qualify your sale as a 1031 exchange.

Installment Sales

If you have to sell your property, there's one last technique to ease the tax bite—an installment sale. Installment sales let you defer your tax until you actually receive your payments. Tax is divided among the actual installments and due as you receive them. No payment is necessary the year of the actual sale; you have to receive at least one payment in a year after the year of the sale. Installment sales aren't available for stock or publicly traded securities. But they're great for "big ticket" sales like businesses and real estate.

The basic concept is simple. First, determine your profit on the sale. Next, determine what percent of the sale price consists of gain. Finally, multiply each installment by your profit percentage to determine taxable gain from that installment. For example, if you buy a building for $600,000, and sell it for $1 million, 40% of your sale price is gain, so 40% of each installment is taxed as capital gain. Here are some rules for some extra wrinkles:

- You have to charge interest on future installments or a portion of each installment will be treated as interest, taxed at ordinary rates, rather than as a capital gain. The minimum rate you have to charge is the applicable federal rate, (published monthly by the Treasury) or 9%

compounded semiannually, whichever is less. Interest you earn on unpaid installments is taxed as ordinary income.

- If you sell a property on which you've claimed depreciation, the entire depreciation is recaptured in the year of the sale. Recapture is taxed as ordinary income, except for real property, which is taxed at no more than 25%.
- You can't use the installment method to sell depreciable property to a business you control or a to trust with you or your spouse as a beneficiary.
- If you sell property with no fixed price—as with an "earnout" sale of a business or rental property for a fixed percentage of sales or rent—divide the property's basis into the term of the installments, then pay tax on any gain above that amount.
- If the total of installment payments owed to you in any year tops $5 million, you'll owe interest at the federal underpayment rate on the balance exceeding $5 million. (We should all have such problems.)
- If your buyer assumes a mortgage, subtract the mortgage amount from the gross sale price before figuring gain on the sale.
- If you elect installment treatment on a sale to a relative (spouse, child, grandchild, parent, grandparent, or sibling) and the relative sells the property within two years of the original sale date (except for death or involuntary conversion), you'll owe tax on the entire remaining gain (minus any loss on the related party's sale).
- Report installment sales on *Form 6252.*

Let's say that in 1990, you buy a rental duplex for $50,000. Over the years, you depreciate $7,180. In 1998, you sell it for $100,000, payable in five installments of $20,000 plus 9% interest on the unpaid balance. Your gain is $50,000, or 50% of the sale price. Each $20,000 installment includes $10,000 of taxable gain. You'll also owe recapture on the $7,180 in 1998, plus ordinary income tax on the interest as you earn it.

Rental Real Estate Loss Allowance

Tax-sheltered income is attractive enough by itself. However, many real estate ventures show a loss after depreciation. If your AGI is $150,000 or less, you can deduct up to $25,000 in losses from property you help actively manage. (The loss allowance phases out by 50 cents for each dollar of AGI between $100,000 and $150,000. For purposes of this allowance, AGI does not include Social Security or railroad retirement benefits, and is not reduced by IRA contributions or the exclusion for savings bond interest used to pay higher education expenses.) Let's say your AGI from salary is $80,000. You also manage two apartments in a building you own. The apartments pay you $200 a month after you've paid all your expenses. Depreciation is $300 a month. You pocket the $200, plus take a $100 loss to offset your salary. Here's how to qualify for the allowance:

- You have to actively participate in managing the property.
- You have to net out losses first against other real estate in which you materially participate, then any other passive income, before using the allowance.
- The allowance isn't available to married couples filing separately.
- You can carry forward a loss disallowed by the allowance phaseout.
- The allowance isn't available for six specific uses treated as businesses rather than rental real estate:
    - incidental rentals of property, where the main reason for holding the property is to profit from the gain and the rental income is less than 2% of the property's value,
    - short-term rentals averaging seven days or less,
    - rentals averaging between seven and 30 days where you provide significant personal service,
    - rentals involving "extraordinary personal service," such as nursing homes,

- rentals to a partnership or S corporation not engaged in the business of renting property (such as renting an office building to your S corporation or medical partnership), or
- property opened for use of customers during regular business hours (such as a golf course or swimming pool).

3.3.2 Buying and Owning Real Estate

There are three main ways to own investment real estate: directly, through limited partnerships, and through real estate stocks. Each has advantages and disadvantages depending on how actively you want to manage your property.

Direct Ownership

Direct ownership—owning property in your own name, or perhaps jointly with your spouse—brings with it responsibility to manage and maintain your property. This can mean the headaches of being a landlord—the 3:00 a.m. phone calls, unexpected repairs, and deadbeat tenants. Or it could mean hiring a management firm to handle day-to-day chores for a cut of the income. Direct ownership also qualifies you for the rental real estate loss allowance.

Direct ownership may be appropriate for turning today's rental into tomorrow's retirement home, particularly if you plan to relocate to a popular resort locale. If you can afford it, consider buying your retirement home now. If you can't afford to use it as a vacation home, hire a management company to rent it out. As long as you're involved in approving repairs and tenants, you'll be considered to actively participate to qualify for the rental real estate loss allowance. Retiring to the property will convert it into your primary residence, qualifying you for an extra $250,000 tax-free exclusion for home sales. (See *Chapter 3.3.4,* "Your Home and Your Vacation Home.")

Direct ownership is best for hands-on investors willing to work as landlords (or hire a manager) in exchange for real estate's superior leverage and tax breaks.

Limited Partnerships

A limited partnership is an investment pool involving a general partner, who organizes and manages the investment, and limited partners, who contribute capital and don't manage the investment. The limited partners' financial liability is limited to their actual investment—hence the name *limited* partnership. Publicly offered limited partnerships are generally offered in units of $2,000 and up. These are often organized as blind pools, where the manager doesn't know what properties will be acquired. A limited partnership doesn't pay tax itself. Instead, income and expenses are passed through directly to the partners. A limited partnership thus gives investors much the same tax benefits of direct ownership.

Partnerships are best for hands-off investors who don't actually want to manage property themselves. They offer most of the same tax breaks that you'd get with direct ownership.

Real Estate Stocks

Real estate stocks are publicly traded companies that develop and manage real estate. There are two broad categories of real estate stocks: real estate investment trusts (REITs), and other real estate companies. Each has different tax consequences.

A real estate investment trust is a publicly traded company that buys and manages property and mortgages. Equity REITs buy actual properties; mortgage REITs buy mortgages; and hybrid REITs buy both. There are even golf course and trailer park REITs. Investors who want to buy commercial property—office parks, industrial parks, shopping centers, and large apartment complexes—often can't invest enough to buy it directly themselves. What's more, these properties require a tremendous amount of specialized management expertise. REITs let you buy these properties with many of the same advantages of mutual funds: professional management, instant liquidity, and better diversification than smaller investors could achieve on their own. Some REITs even pay tax-free income. Here's how:

- REITs have to pass through at least 95% of their earnings to shareholders in order to avoid corporate income tax. This means most REITs pay high current income. Over the past 10 years, REITs have paid just under 70% of their total return in current income. This figure varies from year to year, though. For example, in 1986, REITs paid just 17.2% of total return in current income.
- REITs pay income dividends, capital gains dividends, and return of capital dividends. Income dividends are taxed as ordinary income. Capital gains dividends are taxable at long-term capital gains regardless of how long you've held the REIT shares. Return of capital dividends are tax-free income that reduce your basis in the REIT.
- REITs that pay high current income, without offsetting depreciation deductions, may be best suited for tax-deferred accounts such as IRAs. Also, many variable life and annuity providers are adding REIT funds to their investment options.

REITs don't give you the same direct leverage and tax breaks as direct ownership. But their pass-through structure lets them pay higher income than if they paid corporate income tax themselves. REITs are best for hands-off investors who want to include some real estate in their holdings. They're also the most liquid way to own real estate.

If you like the liquidity of REITs, but don't like the high current dividend, consider other real estate stocks. Homebuilders, natural resources developers, and even ski resorts and retailers all own large portfolios of real estate. These companies let you gain from the underlying real estate's appreciation. At the same time, they're not required to pay out such high earnings. This lets them return more to you in the form of tax-advantaged capital gains.

3.3.3 Real Estate Tax Credits

Low-income housing and rehabilitation tax credits are special opportunities for real estate investors. Tax credits are better than write-offs because they cut your tax bill, not your taxable income. There's no material participation test to meet and no at-risk rules to worry about.

Congress created the low-income housing tax credit in 1986 (at the same time it limited other real estate investments) to encourage private development of low-income housing. These are usually suburban and small-town senior citizen apartments—a far cry from the inner-city public housing most of us picture when we think of low-income housing. These investments are usually organized as limited partnerships. The manager buys or builds apartments to operate as low-income housing for 15 years under strict federal rules. The Treasury Department pre-allocates and pre-funds 10 years of tax credits equal to 9 cents for each dollar invested. Once the 15-year period expires, the manager's usual goal is to sell the property and split any appreciation with the investors.

Low-income housing tax credits aren't comparable to the disastrous real estate limited partnerships of the 1980s. Those partnerships were designed to throw off tax deductions, often equaling more than the original investment. Congress changed the rules in the middle of the game, denying deductions and lowering tax rates so the deductions were worth less. Low-income housing tax credits, in contrast, are pre-allocated, pre-funded, so

Congress can't pull the plug. What's more, they don't depend on high tax rates for their value.

You can use low-income housing tax credits to shelter up to $25,000 in taxable income. That means investors in the 15% bracket can cut $3,750 off their total tax. Investors in the 39.6% bracket can cut $9,900. Let's say that you're a married couple with $100,000 taxable income. You'd like to buy a tax credit partnership that paying an annual credit equal to 12% of your investment. The most that you can shelter is $7,000 (28% of $25,000). The most that you should invest is $58,333 ($7,000 divided by .12 yields a $58,333). Of course, your income may change while you own the partnership. Excess credits are wasted, so don't buy more than you need to take the maximum credit.

- You can't use low-income housing tax credits to reduce your tax below the alternative minimum tax. (Corporations can shelter a virtually unlimited amount of income. In fact, corporations are the biggest tax-credit buyers. About two-thirds of the S&P 500 corporations own tax credits, often as much as tens-of-millions-of-dollars worth.)
- Tax credit investments are limited to qualified investors. Depending on state law, you may need a net worth of $150,000, excluding your home and personal property, or a net worth and annual income of $45,000.
- You can't claim the credit if you're married filing separately.
- Tax credits cut your $25,000 rental real estate loss allowance by one dollar for each dollar of credit you claim. For example, if you claim $2,000 in low-income housing tax credits, your $25,000 rental real estate loss allowance is cut to $23,000.
- Low-income housing tax credits distributed by a partnership may also generate passive income and losses to offset other passive investments. This is usually the case when the manager uses leverage to boost the tax credit for each dollar invested. This is even more valuable if you have passive income generators. The passive losses from the partner-

ship can shelter your passive income, while the tax credits cut your tax on other income.

Tax credits can be even more valuable if you're retired. If you've finished raising your kids and paid off your house, you might not have enough deductions to itemize. Since tax credits don't depend on itemizing for their value, they are even more valuable for these investors. Also, tax credits, unlike municipal bonds, don't add to your provisional income for purposes of taxing your Social Security benefits.

The rehabilitation tax credit is similar to the low-income housing tax credit. It's available for certified historic structures and nonresidential pre-1936 buildings. The minimum rehabilitation expense is $5,000 or your adjusted basis in the building, whichever is greater. The credit itself is equal to 10% of rehabilitation expenses.

3.3.4 Your Home/Your Vacation Home

It's become fashionable today to deny that a house is anything more than a home. This may be news to those who lived through the inflationary 1970s and saw the value of their homes soar skyward. An entire generation saw their home as an investment. It's been a long time since most of the nation saw those sorts of gains, and in some areas, home prices are even falling. But residential real estate is still a key investment for most families. U.S. Department of Commerce data indicates that since 1960, residential real estate has gained 6.43% per year. (The U.S. Housing Price Index measures the median sale price of new, privately-owned nonfarm one-family housing units sold in the U.S., with growth reinvested. Of course, the three most important rules in real estate are still "location, location, location." That's nearly 2% better than inflation, which clocked in at 4.51% for the same period. That appreciation, coupled with the mortgage interest deduction and $250,000/$500,000 exclusion from interest for home sale gains, make a dynamite combination for most families.

The key to residential gains, as with investment real estate, is leverage. If you put $10,000 down to buy a $100,000 house, and the value of the house rises just 2% the next year, you might think your investment is a dog. But remember, your actual equity grows from $10,000 to $12,000. That 20% gain is nobody's dog.

Let's quickly review tax rules regarding your home:

- You can deduct interest on up to $1 million of "acquisition indebtedness" you use to buy your primary residence and one additional residence. Loans you use to substantially improve your home also qualify as acquisition indebtedness.
- You can deduct interest on up to $1 million of home construction loans for 24 months from the time construction begins. Interest before and after this period is nondeductible personal interest.
- Your lender will report the interest you pay on Form 1098. This form also goes to the IRS. Check the amount your lender reports to make sure it's correct. If not, contact your lender and have them issue a revised form. If the amounts that you and your lender report don't agree, the IRS may question your return. You can deduct points you pay to buy or improve your primary residence if charging points is an established practice in your geographical area, and the points charged don't exceed the points generally charged in the area. The amount has to be figured as a percentage of the loan amount and specifically itemized as points, loan origination fee, or loan discount fee. Finally, you have to pay the points directly to the lender. If your points don't meet these tests, you can still amortize them over the life of the loan. Your lender will report the amount of deductible points on Form 1098.If you miss a payment and pay a late fee, your late fee is tax-deductible. Prepayment penalties are also deductible.

You probably won't ever pay a dime in tax on home sale gains. That's because you can exclude the first $250,000 in gains from your income ($500,000 for joint filers). This exclusion makes home equity gains more valuable than other gains, and makes a home a better investment. The exclusion also makes it easier to tap your home's equity for retirement income. You don't have to reinvest your gains $125,000 to avoid tax. This lets you convert up to $250,000 of gain ($500,000 for joint filers) and place it into income-producing investments.

If you want to draw down your equity *without* selling your home, consider a reverse mortgage—a loan against your home that let's you draw income today and remain in the home. You can choose a lump sum, periodic payments, or a line of credit. Since the cash you receive is a loan, there's no income tax. Early reverse mortgage lenders have been criticized for inadequate disclosures and unconscionably high fees. But the FHA and Fannie Mae have become involved, and the American Association of Retired People (AARP) has forced better disclosure for its constituents, who make up the majority of borrowers.

You can also profit from a vacation home as an investment. You can earn tax-advantaged income from renting the property. And after you sell your suburban split-level, you can convert your vacation home into your primary home to capture the $250,000 exclusion twice.

If you do choose to treat your home or vacation home equity as part of your investment portfolio, play it safe. Estimate its value at the low end of the possible range, and don't obsess over quarterly or even annual price changes in your area. Houses are tough to value, and tough to sell. Counting on your home to deliver any specific return—particularly years or even decades after you buy—is a recipe for disappointment.

3.4   Options and Futures

Options and futures are derivatives—investments whose values are derived from some underlying security. Options and futures are created to control risk. But ironically, most buyers don't use them to *control* risk at all—they use them to *magnify* it in hope of outsized gains. In my first book, *The 60 Minute Tax Planner*, I described options and futures as the crack cocaine of the investment world, and said that if riverboat gambling hasn't found its way to a state near you, they could help fill that void in your life. The financial media is full of ads for get-rich-quick systems. Of course, if it sounds too good to be true, it probably is.

Options

An option gives you the *right*—but not the *obligation*—to buy or sell an asset at an agreed price (the strike price) by a specified time (the expiration date). Buying a call—going long, in Wall Street parlance—gives you the right to buy someone else's asset. Writing, or selling, a call—going short—gives the option buyer the right to buy *your* asset. Buying a put gives you the right to sell your asset, while selling a put gives the put buyer the right to sell you *their* asset. If you write an option to sell something you already own, you're said to be covered. If you write an option to sell something you *don't* already own, you're said to be naked. This isn't nearly as sexy as it sounds. It's a good way to lose a ton of money in a heartbeat. (I have to confess here that the first time I traded options—in this case, going long an OEX put—I lost 40% of my position in the time it took to eat lunch. I should have at least had a cocktail or two!)

Let's say that Microsplat trades today at $110. You might buy a call that gives you the right to buy 100 shares within the next 90 days at $120 per share. If the share price stays below $120, your call expires worthless and you lose the price of the option. If the share price rises above $120 and you exercise the option and buy the stock, your gain equals the stock price, minus the $120 strike price, minus the option price.

Gains and losses from stock options and equity options—those based on an underlying stock or group of stocks—are taxed as short- or long-term gain and loss, depending on how long you hold the position. Gains from non-equity options—those that trade on a national securities exchange or commodity futures exchange (options on regulated futures contracts and index options) are taxed as Section 1256 contracts. If you hold a non-equity option long on the last day of the year, the mark-to-market rules require you to pay tax for that year as if you had sold your position that day. 60% of your gain or loss will be treated as short-term gain or loss; the remaining 40% will be treated as long-term gain or loss. This long-term treatment gives you a small break. For taxpayers in the 28% bracket, it cuts your actual tax from 28% to 24.8%; for taxpayers in the 39.6% bracket, it cuts your actual tax from 39.6% to 31.76%.

Here are three specific options strategies for tax-efficient investors:

- You can use put options to protect stock profits without selling and paying tax on your gain. Let's say you have $100,000 worth of Microsplat with a cost basis of just $20,000. If you sell, you'll owe up to $16,000 in federal income tax alone. You can buy a put that will rise in value and protect your gain if the price of Microsplat drops. Hold the stock as long as you like, secure in knowing the option "insures" your stock against a fall. You can sell the stock in pieces, or you can borrow against its value. Of course, the insurance has a cost. But the premium you pay for the option can be far less than the tax you would pay if you sold.

- You can write covered calls to earn tax-advantaged extra income. Covered call writing is selling options to buy stock that you already hold. You collect the premium as extra income when you write the option. Your main risk is that the price of your stock will rise and it will be called away from you. However, if you're not willing to actually sell the stock, you can always buy back the option (at a presumably higher price due to the rise in the underlying stock). If the option expires unexercised, your premium is taxable as short-term capital gain in the year the option expires. This can let you collect a premium this year and delay recognizing taxable income until next year. If the option is exercised and you deliver the underlying stock, the premium is added to the sale price and taxed as short or long-term gain depending on your holding period for the underlying stock. This can let you convert the option premium into long-term gain depending on your holding period.

- *Long-Term Equity AnticiPation Securities*, or LEAPS, are long-term options traded on the American Stock Exchange. These let you lock in a buy or sell price for as long as three years, far longer than the bulk of options. And they let you control more shares for less money. Of course, the premium you pay to buy these options is naturally higher.

Futures

A future is an agreement to buy or sell an asset now for future delivery. Futures, unlike options, *require* you to accept or tender delivery. (You can always sell the contract before expiration to avoid actual pork bellies from showing up at your door.) You can use futures to lock in today's price for assets you'll need tomorrow. Or you can use them to speculate on prices. Commodity producers buy and sell futures to hedge their exposure to changing prices. Speculators who shout themselves hoarse in New York and Chicago pits use them to make an old-fashioned killing.

Most individual investors have no business buying individual contracts. If you really want to play this game, find a managed futures program. These are essentially mutual funds for futures, with experienced managers and institutional clout. And many brokers sell principal protection programs which invest a majority of your investments in low-risk Treasuries to guarantee return of your original investment, then use the rest for speculation.

If you'd like to track markets more closely than with traditional index funds, but with less leverage than futures, consider exchange-traded funds. See *Chapter 4.1.2.*

3.5 Commodities

Commodities are agricultural and natural resources—the raw ingredients of finished products and the fuels that drive our economy. There are five main categories of commodities: energy, agriculture, livestock, industrial metals, and precious metals. Commodities are a distinct equity asset subclass. Since they don't move in lockstep with stock markets, you can use them to diversify their holdings. During the high-inflation 1970s, commodities shined. During the disinflationary early 1980s, they lagged. And during the low inflation years since 1986, commodities have paralleled other markets. Commodity prices are also influenced by fundamental factors of supply and demand. As world economies heat up and former third-world nations modernize, many experts expect commodity prices to rise.

There are several ways to buy commodities, depending on the leverage you seek:

- You can buy commodity options and futures directly, like Dan Aykroyd and Eddie Murphy in the movie *Trading Places*. These are highly leveraged, high-risk investments that require special expertise and attention.
- You can give your money to a commodity-trading advisor, who functions much like a mutual fund manager. These funds are generally

organized as limited partnerships, with little liquidity and often high suitability requirements. Most of these are also highly leveraged.

- Many brokerages offer principal protection programs. These are a sub-class of commodity trading funds that invest a majority of your investments in low-risk Treasuries to guarantee return of your original investment, then use the rest to speculate on commodities.

- Finally, you can buy mutual funds. Several fund families offer domestic and global natural resources funds that invest in the commodity producers. These aren't pure commodity plays. General stock market moves will affect these funds as well as commodity price movements. You'll also feel the effects of industry developments like the recent Exxon/Mobil merger. Oppenheimer Funds offers their *Oppenheimer Real Asset Fund* loosely modeled after the Goldman Sachs Commodities Index. The fund offers commodity exposure without the leverage typical of commodity investments. Instead, the fund buys commodity-linked notes whose final payments are linked to commodity prices. If the fund attracts significant assets, other fund families are likely to introduce similar offerings.

Gold is the most popular commodity because of its reputation as an inflation hedge. Other investors like it as life insurance for their stock and bond portfolios. Since gold is so popular, there are several different ways to buy it. All of them carry different tax twists:

- You can buy gold coins or certificates. These don't produce current income, so they're extremely tax-efficient.

- You can buy gold mining stocks and mutual funds. These are taxed like any other stocks or funds. But their prices generally magnify moves in actual gold prices, leveraging your investment.

- Finally, you can buy options and futures. These give you the greatest leverage in exchange for the least tax efficiency. If you're buying gold as a long-term inflation hedge, buy coins, bars, or funds. If you're looking to leverage short-term price moves, buy options or futures.

3.6 Collectibles

Collectibles include a variety of investments whose values are based on quality or scarcity. These range from the finest art and antiques, auctioned at Christie's and Sotheby's, all the way down to bean-bag stuffed animals, given away by the truckload to sell children's hamburgers.

Collectibles have a unique tax twist: capital gains are still taxed at pre-1997 rates. Long-term gains are taxed at 15% for investors in the 15% bracket and capped at 28% for taxpayers in higher brackets. That means there's no tax relief for the vast majority of investors in the 15% and 28% brackets.

Collectibles aren't for amateurs. There's little liquidity, and transaction costs are high. You need to be an expert—or be advised by one—to profit from most collectibles. But if you know your stuff, the psychic rewards can match the money.

If you bought into the Beanie Baby craze and haven't yet sold, you'll be glad to know that you can still deduct losses after the bubble bursts. I suspect that someday they'll qualify as abandoned property, deductible at your cost basis in the year you give them to your nieces and nephews.

3.7 Tax Shelters

Traditional tax shelters were investment pools designed to produce taxable losses to shelter ordinary income. When tax rates ranged up to 90%, saving taxes became even more important than making money. Promoters packaged oil and gas wells, equipment leasing syndicates, cattle breeding and feeding pools, and master recordings—skimming off huge fees for themselves. Brokers sold them at fat 8% commissions. Buyers wrote off their entire investment the first year and continued writing off loses after that. Naturally, it was all too good to last.

Congress slaughtered the classic tax shelters with the 1986 tax reform. They dropped marginal rates to the point where it no longer made sense to lose a dollar to save 28 cents in tax. They imposed new passive activity and at-risk rules that limited taxpayers' ability to write off losses from activities in which they don't materially participate. They limited investors' losses to amounts actually at risk. And they closed most of the loopholes that let U.S. investors use offshore accounts to avoid U.S. taxes.

Today's tax shelters are designed to produce tax-advantaged income. Real estate and equipment leasing ventures take advantage of depreciation deductions to cut tax on rental income. Oil and gas deals take advantage of liberal rules allowing them to deduct depreciation, depletion, and intangible drilling and development costs.

Oil and Gas

Oil and gas programs include exploratory programs that search for new resources, development programs that drill in areas with proven deposits, income programs that purchase existing reserves, and combination programs. These programs carry three main tax advantages:

- You can write off intangible drilling and development costs, such as labor, fuel, and supplies necessary to drill a well. These are deductible as current expenses even if there's no income. This deduction is limited to your amount at-risk in the program.

- You can write off the cost of capital equipment that you use to extract the resources. You can also write off the interest that you pay to borrow capital.
- You can deduct a percentage of the income you earn from the program as a depletion allowance to reflect the economic reality that someday the well will run dry. With cost depletion, you divide the estimated total barrels of oil or cubic feet of gas recoverable from the property into its adjusted basis to determine a per-unit allowance. Then multiply that allowance by the number of barrels or cubic feet sold in a year. With percentage depletion, you can deduct 15% of the gross income from the property, up to 50% of net income or 65% of your taxable income. Use whichever method gives you the biggest deduction.

Most oil and gas programs are organized as limited partnerships. These are generally structured so that your entire investment is deductible the first year (in the form of intangible drilling & development costs) and a portion of your income is returned in the form of tax-advantaged depreciation and depletion. The general partner will supply you with a Form K-1 reporting your share of income and deductions. These partnerships are subject to the passive loss and at-risk rules. You can also buy a working interest in an oil or gas well to avoid the passive loss rule and deduct program expenses against ordinary income.

These programs make the most sense for aggressive long-term investors. Congress hands out the tax breaks in part because oil and gas are risky, and risky means that you can lose your shirt. You don't just have to strike oil—you have to do it when prices are high enough to assure a profit. And the industry still has more than its fair share of fast-talking con men and dubious promoters. If you're still interested, here some issues to consider when you evaluate a deal:

- What is the sponsor's track record? Have they made money for investors?

- Does the sponsor have enough capital to accomplish his goal? In other word, does he have enough money to keep drilling until he strikes oil?
- Are fees reasonable? Oil and gas sponsors aren't like your neighborhood barber who takes a little off the top. Brokers' commissions and sponsors' fees can eat up to 25% of your original investment. The prospectus will tell you exactly how much the broker and sponsor get, whether you strike oil or not.

Equipment Leasing

Equipment leasing programs buy equipment such as computers, machine tools, airplanes, railroad cars, and ships, to lease to eventual users. Their main tax strategy is depreciation. The Modified Accelerated Cost Recovery System introduced in 1986 lets equipment buyers front-load their depreciation deduction for fatter deductions their first few years of ownership. This depreciation, along with up-front costs and interest on any borrowed capital, shelters your income the first years of the lease. Most equipment leasing ventures are organized as limited partnerships. The general partner will supply you with a Form K-1 reporting your share of income and deductions from the program.

These programs are appropriate for the same investors who might buy oil and gas. They're safer because cash flows are more predictable. But you don't always know what the equipment will be worth at the end of the term. And the same cautions about track records and fees apply.

Offshore Opportunities

Offshore opportunities include bank accounts, investment accounts, partnerships and corporations in foreign countries. Many investors believe they can use offshore accounts to avoid U.S. tax. But Congress has closed most of the loopholes that once let U.S. investors expatriate their money to avoid taxes. Today, you owe tax on any income you receive from offshore accounts, as well as offshore trusts that you establish with U.S. beneficiaries. You also have to report any such accounts with more than $10,000 in assets on your Schedule B. The IRS and Treasury Department take these requirements very seriously.

Some hedge funds and other investment pools operate offshore to avoid U.S. reporting requirements. Those requirements exist for your protection. Think carefully before you waive them. The main reason to move offshore is to protect your assets from U.S. courts and creditors. But even these protections are crumbling. In 1999, the U.S. District Court for the Southern District of California, and the Sixth Circuit Court of Appeals conceded that they might not have jurisdiction over assets a Las Vegas couple transferred to a Cook Islands trust. But the courts did choose to exercise their jurisdiction over the couple themselves by tossing them in jail until they coughed up gains from a telemarketing scam.

If you're interested in offshore opportunities, and you have access to the Internet, you simply *must* see attorney Jay Adkisson's web site at *www.falc.com*. Adkission is a litigator—not a tax planner—who specializes in exposing fraud, both onshore and off. He skewers the bad guys by name. Great fun! You should also consult IRS Publication 2193, "Too Good to be True Trusts."

3.8   Avoid Tax on Capital Gains

One of the most common dilemmas you might face is a large position in a single investment with a low basis. It may be a stock, a business, or rental real estate. You want to sell—to diversify, to put your grandchild through college, or to cruise around the world. But you don't want to pay a whopping tax bill. Which is worse: the market risk of holding an oversized position, or the certainty of paying tax?

One solution to the problem of a single large holding is to buy insurance in the form of a put—an option giving you the right, but not the obligation, to sell the stock ("put" it to the option seller) at a predetermined price. The put lets you rest confident in the knowledge that, even if the stock tanks, you'll be protected. But puts, like any other insurance, cost money. One study showed the annualized cost of holding a put on a blue chip stock at between 12-18% of the stock's price. (If your puts expire worthless, you can deduct their cost, plus commissions, as capital losses in the year the put expires.)

If you sell your stock, you'll get the benefit of long-term capital gain rates. But there are several advanced strategies you can use to minimize or avoid capital gains on stocks or similar low-basis investments.

3.8.1 Borrow Against Your Assets

The easiest way to avoid tax on your gain is not to sell. The problem, of course, is that this keeps your equity locked in your asset. But you can still tap your equity without triggering tax. You can use your home, your investment real estate, and even your securities as collateral for a loan or line of credit. You can also borrow against a permanent life insurance policy. This accomplishes two goals. First, you gain access to your principal and your gains. Second, your asset continues to appreciate.

Many investors are reluctant to margin their securities, or borrow against them, out of fear of a stock market crash. In the 1920s, brokers loaned customers up to 90% of the value of their stocks. This level of debt turned many long-term investors into leveraged speculators. When the crash came, it took relatively small declines to wipe out their entire equity. Lenders hit borrowers with margin calls—demands for more cash to protect their security interests. Borrowers couldn't pay, so the lenders sold them out, driving prices even lower. That's why your grandmother keeps her money in the bank.

But you can borrow without exposing yourself to that sort of risk. Brokers and bankers will generally lend up to 50% of the value of your stocks, 80% of mutual funds, and 98% of Treasury securities. Some specialized lenders will set up hedges letting you borrow up to 90% of your stock's value (See **Chapter 3.8.6**, "Tax-Engineered Products.") You don't have to pay periodic interest—instead, it's added to your debt. This gives you complete flexibility to repay the loan on your terms.

It makes sense to keep at least a part of your investment in taxable accounts just for emergency borrowing. There's no application, no credit check, no income verification, and no fees. Margin rates are usually lower than anything else but a mortgage. Life insurance agents rightly tout the tax advantages of borrowing against a policy's cash value. But most investors don't know they can also take the same advantage from most taxable investments.

3.8.2 Year-end Planning

There are several year-end moves you can make to help avoid or reduce tax on appreciated assets:

- Deferring the sale doesn't avoid tax, but at least delays it. Delaying tax actually cuts your tax by letting you pay with less valuable future dollars.
- You can sell a position over time. There's no law that says you have to sell it all at once.
- You can also use a version of this strategy in reverse if your tax rate this year is lower than it will be in future years. Sell now, to pay tax on the current gain at today's low rate. Then, repurchase to increase your basis

before taking gains tomorrow at your higher rate. Let's say you're between jobs, and this year you're likely to be in the 15% bracket. Next year, when you find a job, you'll be in the 28% bracket. You have 1,000 shares of Microsplat you bought two years ago for $10 per share. It's worth $20 now, and you're hoping to sell it next year at $25. Consider selling the stock now, in the low-bracket year, and immediately buying it back. Your capital gain rate on the increase from $10 to $20 this year will be 10%, half as much as next year's rate of 20%. By selling this year, you pay $1,000—10% of the $10,000 gain. If you wait and sell it at the same price next year, your tax would be $2,000—20% of the same $10,000 gain. Even if you resell it next year for more than $20 per share, you'll have cut your tax on the portion of your gain between $10 and $20 per share. (Before you try this, determine how much gain you can take without pushing yourself into a higher bracket. And don't do it if you aren't completely confident the stock will keep rising.)

3.8.3 Tax Swaps

A tax swap is when you sell an asset at a loss and replace it with a similar—but not identical—investment. Your portfolio looks the same—but you get to book the loss on your original asset. This makes sense when the tax savings are larger than the transaction costs. You can use tax swaps with individual securities, mutual funds, and even real estate. For example, you can swap one computer company for another, one growth fund for another, or one apartment for another. If you buy back your original investment within 31 days before or after the original sale, your loss (but not any gain) will be disallowed as a wash sale. Buying back shares in the same security counts as buying your original asset.

If you want to keep your same investment and still realize a loss, you can use a strategy called doubling up. This involves buying an identical lot more than 31 days before selling your old lot. You can also use your IRA to avoid the wash sale rule. Sell an investment from a taxable account, and buy it back in your IRA. The taxable account lets you take the loss, but buying it back in an IRA is not the same as buying it back yourself. If the asset's value continues to fall, you can't deduct the extra loss from the IRA.

3.8.4 Gifts

If you have an asset that you wish to sell to benefit a lower-bracket tax-payer, such as a child or parent, consider giving them the asset and letting them sell it. They will receive the gift with a carryover basis equal to your basis in the asset. When they sell, they then pay tax on the appreciation at their lower bracket. This saves the difference between their tax and yours. This strategy is especially useful for paying college tuition. Giving an asset to your college-age child will nearly always result in less tax than if you sell it yourself.

3.8.5 Charitable Gifts

Charitable gifts of appreciated property let you do good for others while you do well for yourself. When you give a gift of appreciated property (stocks, mutual funds, real estate, or artwork) held for more than a year, you can deduct the property's full market value and avoid paying tax on your capital gain.

• First you'll need to determine the value of property you donate. With securities, fair market value is the average of the high and low sale prices on the date of the donation. With real estate and works of art, you'll need an appraisal. The IRS retains an Art Advisory Board to help decide whether to accept or contest these valuations. Appraisal fees are a miscellaneous itemized deduction subject to the 2% floor.

- You have to hold the property for at least a year to deduct the fair market value. If you hold the property yourself for less than a year, you can deduct only your purchase price.
- Make sure the charity sells the property, not you. If you sell it in your own name, then donate the proceeds, you'll still owe the tax on the capital gain.
- You can deduct up to 30% of your AGI for gifts of appreciated property to public charities and qualifying private foundations. You can carry over any unused deduction for up to five years.
- There's no deduction for gifts of property worth less than when you bought it.
- You can deduct up to 30% of your AGI for gifts of appreciated property (20% for gifts of appreciated property to private foundations). If your gift exceeds 30% of your AGI, you can carry the remaining deduction to future years.

Charitable giving is one of the most effective tax planning strategies left. But watch out! There's no shortage of dubious promotions and out-and-out cons waiting to catch your dollars! The IRS recently shot down a popular scheme involving charitable split-dollar life insurance. It worked like this: 1) you gave money to the charity and took an immediate deduction (nice!), 2) the charity bought an insurance policy on your life, and, 3) at your death, your heirs got most of the insurance proceeds. It sounded too good to be true—and it was. Thousands of donors are likely to wind up owing millions in taxes and penalties.

Charitable Trusts

Charitable trusts are an advanced tool that let you sell appreciated assets and take a substantial deduction while you retain an income from the property, all at the same time. Charitable trusts also offer important estate tax breaks. A trust, in general, is when one party holds property for the benefit of another. The person giving the property is a grantor. The person holding the property is the trustee. And those who get the benefit of the property are beneficiaries. With charitable trusts, you as grantor donate property to yourself or someone else as trustee, for benefit of yourself, your heirs, and one or more charitable organizations. You'll need a lawyer to set one up, but the IRS has published specimen documents to help keep down the cost. Charitable trusts are appropriate for gifts of $100,000 or more, large enough to justify the annual tax return and investment management fees.

There are two main classes of charitable trusts: charitable lead trusts, where the charity gets a stream of income and you or your heirs get the eventual principal; and charitable remainder trusts (CRTs), where you and your family get the income and the charity gets the eventual principal, or remainder. Each class includes two types according to how that income is paid out: annuitrusts, which pay a specific dollar amount, or annuity; and unitrusts, which pay a fixed percentage of the trust's value. Typically, the income lasts until the grantor's death. So, a charitable lead annuitrust, or CLAT, is when you give the income from the trust to the charity, then leave the remainder to your heirs. A charitable remainder unitrust, or CRUT, is when you keep the income for yourself, then leave the remainder to the charity. (If the trust doesn't earn enough to pay the target income in a given year, you can direct the trustee to make up the shortfall from future surpluses. This is called a makeup provision.) Trusts offer these advantages:

- You avoid capital gains tax on property you donate to the trust.
- The trust can trade investments, to pay more income or just diversify holdings, without paying tax on sales.
- You get an immediate charitable deduction for the gift you make to the trust.

- You remove the value of the property you donate from your taxable estate.

Let's say that you and your spouse are both 60 years old. Years ago you bought $50,000 worth of stock. The stock is now worth $200,000 and pays a 2% dividend. You'd like to boost your current income and use the stock to benefit your college. But you don't want to sell and pay $30,000 tax on the gain. Instead, you donate the stock to a CRUT. The trust sells the stock and reinvests in a balanced portfolio yielding 5% per year and growing at another 5%. You keep the 5% income and, at your death, the charity gets the portfolio. This increases your income from $4,000 to $10,000 per year. It avoids capital gains tax on the sale of the stock. And it gives you a charitable deduction equal to the remainder interest you donate to the college.

Your gift will be equal to the fair market value of the property you give, minus the present value of the income you retain. Generally, you determine the present value using standard valuation tables that reflect your life expectancy and the applicable federal rate. The IRS publishes these tables monthly to make sure you use a reasonable interest rate assumption. Your attorney, your CPA, or the charity's development officer can calculate the actual value of your gift.

Your maximum deduction for gifts to charitable trusts is limited to 30% of your AGI. If the value of your gift tops 30% of your AGI, you can carry the excess deduction forward just five years. So it's important to plan correctly and project your future income to make the most of particularly large gifts exceeding 180% of a single year's AGI.

Here are several planning techniques to make the most of charitable trusts:

- You can designate a CRT as your IRA beneficiary. Let's say you have a $1 million IRA balance. At your death, estate taxes can take more than half, and income taxes can take more than 40% of what's left. This can leave as little as $200,000 to benefit your heirs. You can designate a CRT as beneficiary of the IRA, then designate your heirs as the income beneficiaries of the trust. There will be no income tax due on the transfer, and your estate will get a deduction for the present value of the charity's remainder interest. This might cut your estate tax by 25% or more. The net result is to preserve far more principal from which your heirs can draw income.

- Another strategy is to fund the trust with a variable annuity rather than taxable stocks and bonds or funds. This lets you accumulate income without paying tax in years when you have no need for a distribution.
- You can use a CLAT or CLUT as a supplemental retirement plan without burdensome qualified plan rules.
- You can use a "term of years" CLAT to shift income to your children, to be taxed at their lower rate, while you snag a charitable deduction today.

Charitable trusts aren't for amateurs. If this introduction sounds appealing, consult your estate planner, your CPA, or your charity's development officer.

Charitable Trust Alternatives

Here are three alternatives to traditional CRTs:

- A charitable gift annuity is a gift to the charity in exchange for an annuity income for your life. Your deductible gift equals the present value of the charity's remainder interest. The Committee on Gift Annuities, a steering committee of approximately 1,000 organizations, publishes periodic interest rates designed to produce a 50% remainder at your death. The disadvantages of this arrangement, for nervous donors, is that your account isn't segregated as it would be with a charitable trust.

Also, you'll want a financially sound charity capable of making the payments over your life.

- A donor-advised fund is a charitable trust that accepts gifts from multiple donors and invests funds until the donor directs the fund to make an actual contribution. There's no retained income as there is with a trust, pooled income fund, or gift annuity.

- Finally, a private foundation is a perpetual irrevocable trust you establish to accept donations. You don't retain any income as you would with a regular CRT, pooled income fund, or gift annuity. Instead, you select a board of directors, who decides who gets the money. The foundation has to make donations equaling at least 5% of its assets each year. However, if the foundation earns more than that on its principal, the board can use the excess to pay expenses. In fact, some donors use these foundations to give their heirs jobs as trustees. These are appropriate for gifts of $500,000 and up.

3.8.6 Tax-Engineered Products

Tax-engineered products include a constantly changing class of sophisticated strategies for heavy hitters. Most are limited to investors with at least $1 million in a single stock. That's not as much as it used to be. Some of these strategies turn on separating ownership of a stock from any risk. Others involve creating derivative securities whose prices are derived from the underlying asset—usually the stock in question. Let's face it—these are the "loopholes" that politicians are quick to condemn.

"Equity swaps" are one tool that let you lock in profits without selling your stock. Let's say you have $5 million worth of stock in your former company. The stock yields 2%, and pays just $100,000 a year. You'd rather buy some Treasury bonds and make three times that amount. You'd sell the stock to buy the bonds, but there's the small matter of $1 million you'd owe in tax. No problem! You and your broker swap the risks and rewards of owning the actual stock for the income you would earn from the Treasuries. You keep legal title to the stock. Since there's no sale, there's no tax. Sure, you'll pay your broker a fee for the service. But it's far less than you'd pay in tax on the stock.

"Swap funds" are a similar tool for diversifying low-basis stock or other assets without selling. Transferring property into a partnership is generally not a taxable event. That is, there's no capital gains tax on appreciated property you transfer into a partnership. So, you contribute your low-basis stock or other assets into a partnership made up of other wealthy investors. You end up owning shares in a more diversified portfolio consisting of all the investors' various assets. Or the fund itself could sell the assets and invests in a diversified portfolio. The IRS has clamped down on these funds by barring tax-free transfers into partnerships with too much of their assets invested in readily marketable securities, and raising the holding period before the fund can distribute diversified assets back to the partners. Still, they remain useful tools for investors with $1 million or more.

"Zero-cost collars" are a third way to tap your equity and diversify your holdings without actually selling your stock. First, you set up a hedge to protect your position. This involves selling a call, which is an option obligating you to sell the stock at a certain price, and buying a put, which is an option protecting you from a fall in the price. The money you make from selling the call pays for the cost of the put—hence the name "zero-cost" collar. Your biggest danger is the chance that the price of the stock will soar and the call buyer will exercise the option, forcing you to sell and realize the gain. (You could also simply buy the put if you want to hedge your position without the risk of having to sell if the price soars.) Then, simply borrow against the stock, safely knowing the put protects your position. Most lenders will only give you 50% of the stock's value. The collar gives your lender confidence to lend you up to 90%.

Tax-engineered products constantly change with tax and investment policies. If you have $1 million or more in a single stock or asset, have your investment advisor, attorney, or CPA look into these solutions. It could save you tens of thousands in tax.

Chapter 4

Managed Money

Managed money—mutual funds, unit investment trusts, and separate accounts—are the best way for most investors to buy most securities. We'll spend most of this chapter discussing the most popular form of money management, open-ended mutual funds. We'll also cover closed-end funds, unit investment trusts, separate accounts, and hedge funds.

A mutual fund is an investment company that pools money from shareholders and invests in a diversified portfolio. The fund hires a professional manager who invests according to guidelines set forth in a prospectus. Each fund share is worth its proportional piece of the fund's underlying investments. With open-end funds, the bulk of today's offerings, the manager deals directly with shareholders, buying and selling daily according to the day's closing net asset value. With closed-end funds, the manager issues a set number of shares, which then trade on an established market.

Mutual funds, like Mafia dons, work in families. A single family may include up to 100 funds. This variety lets you allocate assets across a broad spectrum of asset classes and styles. You can switch money from one fund into another, usually just with a phone call. If you buy your fund from a broker, and pay a sales commission, you can switch funds within the family without paying additional commission on your original investment.

Mutual funds offer these advantages to both new and experienced investors:

- Funds offer professional management at a reasonable fee. This is an important plus for new investors without the experience to assemble portfolios on their own. It's also valuable for experienced investors venturing into new areas, such as junk bonds or international stocks. Today, over 80% of stock trades are made by institutional investors—mutual funds, pension funds, and endowments. These are the best money managers in the business. Do you want to compete against them? Or hire them to work for you?

- Funds offer instant diversification for a minimal investment. You get a complete portfolio with a single purchase. If you're venturing into a new asset class, you can buy a complete portfolio that you couldn't confidently or economically assemble yourself with individual securities. And some asset classes, such as junk bonds and emerging-markets stocks, just aren't practical for individual investors.

- Funds offer instant liquidity and, in most cases, 24-hour trading access. You can buy and sell at the day's closing net asset value without worrying about spreads, markups, and execution.

- Funds are ideal for IRAs, custodial accounts, and systematic investment plans because you can buy them in bite-size chunks. A $250 or even $1,000 stock investment can't buy enough individual shares of stock to justify the steep commissions for such small purchases.

- Funds are the most convenient way to dollar-cost average. Dollar-cost-averaging is a strategy for buying a set dollar amount of shares at constant intervals regardless of underlying share price, which yields higher average gains per share in rising markets.

- Since so many fund families offer funds with similar objectives, they're ideal for tax swaps.

These investment advantages are so powerful that I recommend mutual funds even though they actually cost you some control over taxes:

- You don't just owe tax when you sell fund shares at a gain—you also owe tax when the manager sells the fund's holdings at a gain. That means your fund manager exercises most control over taxes, choosing which gains to realize and when to do so. The only control you exercise is when you sell the fund. And most funds don't invest with an eye towards after-tax returns. (Index funds and tax-managed funds are two solutions to this problem. See below.)

- You can't separate out your fund's winners from losers, or realize a single underlying holding's gain. For example, you can't carve out a big winner and give those shares to your family charity. (Of course, you can carve out a portion of your fund shares and donate *that*. It makes sense to use low-basis shares for gifts to charity, to avoid capital gains on the appreciation, or gifts to lower-bracket family members, who can then pay tax on the gain at their lower rates.)

- Management fees are an extra expense that you wouldn't pay to buy and hold individual securities. However, as you'll see below, there are funds with management fees that total less than the commission you'd pay to manage your own portfolio.

Today there are more than 10,000 funds: open- and closed-end funds; load funds and no-load funds, stock, bond, and balanced funds; domestic and foreign funds. There are sector funds for every major industry and country funds for every major market. One fund family has introduced a fund that invests in publicly traded companies employing members of the International Association of Machinists. There are socially responsible funds that avoid companies involved in alcohol, tobacco, weapons, and other irresponsible corporate citizens. There's even a socially *irresponsible* fund that buys the good stuff the responsible funds don' (Morgan FunShares, NASDAQ symbol MFUN). As one author has said, "...if the Martians landed on Earth tomorrow, the day after there'd be a mutual fund purporting to take advantage of the trend in interplanetary invasion."

As with so many other investments, the key to mutual fund tax efficiency is the portion of total return that comes from current income and short-term gains versus the portion that comes from long-term capital gains. Money market funds, adjustable-rate funds, and loan participation funds are the least efficient because all of their gain comes from currently taxable income. Taxable bond funds, junk funds, and strategic income funds are also inefficient because the bulk of their total return comes from current income. Stock funds range from efficient index funds to high-tax market neutral funds. Finally, balanced funds, asset allocation funds, and lifestyle funds range from tax misers to tax gluttons.

Most mutual funds pay no tax themselves. Instead, they distribute their income and gains directly to you. These distributions largely determine how much tax you pay on the distributions:

- Income dividends are income earned by the fund's investments—bond interest, stock dividends, and the like. Income dividends may be distributed monthly, quarterly, or annually, depending on how much income the fund's investments generate. Income dividends are taxed as ordinary income whether you take them in cash or reinvest them in more shares. Some dividends, such as from Treasury bond and municipal bond funds, include interest that's partially or fully free from state taxes. If so, the fund will tell you how much to exclude from your state tax return.

- Capital gains dividends are profits from the fund's portfolio. These are generally taxed as long-term capital gains, regardless of how long you own the shares. And, like income dividends, capital gains distributions are taxed when distributed whether you take the distribution in cash or reinvest in more shares. These can come as ugly surprises—and even stick you with a tax bill when the fund itself loses money.

- "Return of capital" distributions are distributions of your own capital. These distributions generally aren't included in taxable income. Instead, they reduce your basis in your shares when you finally sell. If your basis is already down to zero, then report further "return of capital" distributions as capital gains.

- Some funds may retain long-term capital gains and pay tax themselves, rather than distributing those gains to shareholders. You still owe tax on the gain, but you can claim a credit for the tax the fund pays.
- Some funds that invest abroad pay foreign tax on foreign income. You can claim a deduction or a credit for your share of the fund's foreign taxes. To claim the deduction, simply report it on Schedule A, along with state and local income and property taxes. But the credit will usually cut your tax more. If your foreign tax is less than $300 ($600 for joint filers), and your only foreign income is qualified passive income (including mutual fund income), you can claim the credit directly on Form 1040. If your share of the fund's foreign tax is higher than those amounts, determine the credit on *Form 1116.* This involves figuring complicated ratios for different kinds of foreign income. But it beats paying the same tax twice.

The same general rules apply in cutting tax on your funds as with any other investment. First, choose tax-efficient funds. Second, buy and sell your funds efficiently. The bulk of this Chapter tells you how to accomplish these dual goals. Fund investors looking for tax deferral should also consider variable annuities. A variable annuity is a contract with an insurance company offering a group of "subaccounts" that resemble a mutual fund family in a tax-deferred wrapper. Your income grows tax-deferred, and you can make tax-free transfers among subaccounts. In fact, many variable annuity subaccounts are virtual "clones" of popular mutual funds. They are even more useful for sheltering interest income from the fixed-income portion of your portfolio. However, in exchange for tax deferral, variable annuities cost you lower long-term capital gains rates. (See *Chapter 7.2.3*, "Variable Annuities.")

The Internet offers a wealth on information for mutual fund investors. Here are just a few of my favorite sites:

5   Morningstar mutual funds, *www.morningstar.com*, offers original research and commentary on individual stocks as well as mutual

funds. You can screen for stocks and funds according to your own requirements. Most services are free; some require a membership fee. You can also find Morningstar at any decent public library.

6   The *Forbes* magazine web site, ***www.forbes.com/funds***, ranks mutual funds separately for performance in up markets and down. This is helpful if you're looking specifically to profit from market updrafts or protect yourself from downturns.

7   *Smart Money* magazine's mutual fund analyzer, ***www.smart-money.com/intro/funds***, highlights risk, return, fees, and performance. Their "fund portfolio builder" lets you build your own portfolio and analyze its performance and volatility over the past five years.

8   Index Funds Online, ***www.indexfunds.com***, features index fund information and profiles from various sources.

9   The Undiscovered Managers web site, at ***www.undiscoveredman-agers.com***, specializes in discovering "some of the best money managers in the world you've never heard of …until now." They offer outstanding information on mutual funds and taxes, plus overviews and links to behavioral finance research and a special report on the future of money management that is changing the way your financial advisor does business.

10 FundAlarm, at ***www.fundalarm.com***, weeds out funds underperforming their benchmarks for one-, three-, and five-year periods, then adds manager change alerts and more commentary.

4.1   Six Ways to Choose Funds

Here are six ways to choose tax-efficient funds in your taxable accounts. These strategies, along with the buying and selling strategies discussed later, will help cut your fund taxes to the lowest amount appropriate for your individual goals.

If you're buying funds in your tax-deferred account, you should still pay attention to tax efficiency. That's because you need to manage your taxable and tax-deferred accounts as a single portfolio. You'll need to know which funds to buy in the taxable account and which to shelter with tax deferral. (See *Chapter 6.1*, "Tax-Deferred Compounding.")

4.1.1 Index Funds

Most mutual funds hire active managers who try to beat the market in whatever securities they manage. Managers score themselves against an index that tracks the market for their particular securities. Large-cap managers, for example, generally aim to beat the S&P 500, an index of the 500 largest companies by market capitalization. But beating the market, particularly after taxes and expenses, is hard. Indexes don't pay taxes or expenses.

Index funds don't try to beat the market. Instead, they aim to track a particular index. The largest funds do it by buying every security tracked in the index. Smaller funds do it by buying a representative sample, or by buying options on the index. Index funds have exploded in recent years, with more than 200 index funds tracking large-cap, mid-cap and small-cap indexes, foreign indexes, and fixed-income indexes. There's even a fund that purports to track an index of "tombstone" stocks: funeral homes, cemeteries, and casket makers.

Index funds offer these advantages over their actively managed competitors:

- Index funds deliver consistently superior returns. Critics accuse them of guaranteeing mediocrity. But, considering that index funds beat the majority of their actively-managed rivals, indexing is actually more like guaranteeing par. Index proponents aren't likely to score the knockout punch proving indexing unbeatable. But the evidence suggests that in taxable accounts, the rewards of trying to beat the index just aren't worth the cost.

- Index funds are cheap. Since they don't actively try to beat the market, they don't pay the costs of trying: manager's fees, research, and trading costs. Index funds as a group have the lowest expense ratios in the business. The average stock fund, for example, costs 1.47% per year. The average index fund costs just 0.62%, with some funds ranging below 0.20%. That means the average actively managed fund has to beat the average index fund by 0.85% just to break even—*before* paying extra taxes.

- Index funds are the most reliable way to implement asset allocation choices. They don't hold large cash reserves, so performance isn't diluted. And they don't make big bets outside their published objectives. For example, in the spring of 1997, Fidelity Magellan's Jeffrey Vinik, fearing a stock market downturn, made large bets on bonds. He was wrong—and he lost billions for investors who thought they were buying stocks.

True index funds—those that buy the entire index, and hold it—enjoy a huge tax advantage over actively managed funds. Low turnover means low realized capital gains, therefore, low taxable gains. Each time an active fund manager sells a stock at a profit, she generates a capital gain to be distributed and taxed to shareholders. Index funds sell only when necessary to redeem exiting shares or when the index itself changes. Index funds can also hold less cash than active funds since index investors redeem their shares less often. In fact, many index funds limit transfers just to hold down this sort of expensive turnover.

Some index funds don't actually buy their underlying index. Instead, they buy a representative sample to track it. Some funds may use options or futures to track the index or even beat it. These options and futures generate short-term gains—and lots of them. They don't give you the tax advantages of true index funds. So, be careful when you index. Hold true index funds in taxable accounts. Buy proxy index funds, enhanced index funds, and leveraged funds in your IRA or retirement accounts.

Be especially careful before you buy "leveraged" index funds. These are funds that use options or futures to return a multiple of the index's return each day. For example, a leveraged fund might aim to earn 150% of the S&P 500's daily return. This leverage can be a double-edged sword. In down markets, the funds *fall* faster than the index. This means your future gains build back from a lower base. University of Chicago professor Richard Polson has calculated that leveraged funds can lag their index and even lose money when the index rises.

The S&P 500 includes over 70% of the U.S. stock market, by market capitalization. But it certainly isn't the only index out there:

- You can track growth and value indexes. Growth indexes are more efficient because of lower dividends, but also more volatile. This makes sense considering the underlying characteristics of growth and value stocks themselves. (*Morningstar* reports that for the five-year period ending 5/31/98, Vanguard's Index Growth Fund was more tax efficient than their Index Value Fund (96.4% vs. 90.2%), but also more volatile, as measured by standard deviation (17.2% vs. 14.2%.)
- You can track smaller stocks with the Russell 1000 (the largest 1000 companies by market capitalization), the Russell 2000 (the next-largest 2000 stocks by market capitalization, often used as a proxy for small stocks), the Wilshire 4500 (the entire U.S. stock market *minus* the 500 largest companies), and the Wilshire 5000 (the entire U.S. market). You can also track small-cap growth and small-cap value indexes. Some advisors believe indexing is less effective with small stocks because this market is less efficient and there is more room for an active manager to add value. These indexes also have more substitutions, which boosts

turnover and realized capital gains. But the evidence suggests that indexing these markets still adds value by cutting costs and reducing turnover.

- Real estate investors can track the Morgan Stanley REIT index.
- Socially responsible investors can choose three funds tracking custom social indexes. These include the **Domini Social Equity Fund**, the Citizens Fund, and *the Vanguard Calvert Social Index Fund*.
- Commodity buyers can buy the **Oppenheimer Real Asset Fund**, which loosely tracks the Goldman Sachs Commodity Index.
- International investors can track over two dozen developed market, emerging market, and individual country indexes.

The **Vanguard Group** is the clear leader in index fund assets, with over 60% of the market. Vanguard's Index 500 Trust has passed Fidelity's Magellan as the world's largest mutual fund, with over $100 billion in assets. Dozens of fund families have added index funds, with over 50 that track the S&P 500 alone. Even full-service brokers have added funds tracking the S&P 500, the Russell 2000, and the MSCI EAFE, among others. But not all index funds are created equal. Once you've decided to index, pay attention to loads, expense ratios, and other measures of mutual-fund efficiency. The following table reveals just how widely index fund performance can vary. In May, 1999, *The Wall Street Journal* surveyed a dozen S&P 500 funds for the period ending April 30, 1999. Loads ranged from zero to five percent. Annual expenses ranged from 0.18% to a whopping 1.50%. And tax-adjusted returns ranged from 18.28% to 21.10%. Not surprisingly, the fund with the highest tax-adjusted return had the lowest expense.

Index Fund Comparison				
Fund	One-Year Return	Tax-Adj Return	Expense Ratio	Max Load
BlackRock Index Equity Inv. B	20.11%	19.90%	1.38%	4.5%
BT Investment Equity 500 Index	21.71	20.72	0.25	None
Dreyfus S&P 500 Index	21.16	20.68	0.50	None
Harris Insight Index N	21.13	19.46	0.70	None
Mason Street Index 500 Stock A	21.19	20.70	0.85	4.75
Merrill Lynch S&P 500 Index D	21.04	19.55	0.64	None
Morgan Stanley Dean Witter S&P 500 Index	20.15	20.09	1.50	5.0
ProFunds Bull Investors	18.33	18.28	1.33	None
Scudder S&P 500 Index	21.50	21.05	0.40	None
Stagecoach Equity Index B	20.01	18.91	1.45	5.0
Vanguard 500 Index	21.87	21.10	0.18	None
Wachovia Equity Index Y	21.15	19.97	0.45	None
S&P 500	21.83			

Source: Morningstar Mutual Funds, as published in The Wall Street Journal, 5/21/99

Finally, buying index funds and holding them for long-term returns lets you sleep late and ignore the hype of mutual funds marketing. Magazine covers tout "Hot Funds to Buy Now"; market gurus fill newsletters and airwaves with tips. The hype implies that the key to making money is picking the right horse. But as we've seen, most active portfolio management falls short of its promise. Buying an index fund lets you bet on *every* horse.

4.1.2 Exchange-Traded Funds

Exchange-traded funds, or ETFs, are the most exciting new investment vehicle since the variable annuities. I'm confident these funds will give traditional mutual funds a run for their money—as well as enrich thousands of investors without unduly enriching the U.S. Treasury.

There are roughly 100 exchange-traded funds available today. State Street Global Advisors was first out the chute with their popular SPDRs (Standard & Poors Depository Receipts), which track the S&P 500;

Diamonds, which track the Dow Jones; and QQQs (pronounced "cubes"), which track the NASDAQ 100. State Street also sponsors mid-cap SPDRS tracking the S&P mid-cap index and select sector SPDRs tracking specific industry groups. Barclays Global Investors has introduced "iShares," which track international indexes, as well as domestic sectors such as large-cap growth, large-cap value, and the like. And Merrill Lynch has introduced HOLDRS (Holding Company Depository Receipts), which track specified groups of stock in industries such as biotech and broadband communications. Exchange-traded funds generally trade on the American Stock Exchange, and can account for more than half of the AMEX's daily trading volume. The trusts are as good as permanent for today's investors—they're generally not scheduled to terminate until sometime in the 22nd century. Annual expenses are generally lower than similar open-end index funds. For example, you can currently invest $100,000 in the S&P 500 for a management fee of just $80. You probably can't buy a decent pair of *shoes* for that much—let alone world-class investment management.

Exchange-traded funds have several advantages over their traditional open-end cousins:

- You can buy and sell during the trading day without waiting for daily closing prices.
- You can sell short to profits from falling markets. Exchange-traded funds are exempt from the "uptick" rule (which keeps you from shorting stocks except after a price uptick); this lets you short them following a downtick.
- You can buy ETFs with full-service brokerage firms that don't carry no-load mutual funds.
- When other shareholders sell their shares, there's no liquidation forcing the fund to distribute built-in capital gains, as there is with traditional open-end index funds.

- ETFs are particularly good for investing in smaller foreign markets such as Austria and Spain. Previously, you were limited to closed-end country funds with higher expenses.

Exchange-traded funds have disadvantages, too, but none so serious to avoid them:

- You'll have to pay brokerage commissions to buy and sell them. Eight bucks. Big deal.
- Exchange-traded funds can't reinvest their dividend income immediately. They generally deposit dividends into noninterest-bearing accounts and reinvest them quarterly. This leads to a condition called "dividend cash drag," which causes the exchange-traded fund to lag behind a traditional index fund. However, Barclays plans to solve this problem by lending securities to short-sellers and investing undistributed dividends into income-paying repurchase agreements and futures.

Your mother always told you that you can judge someone by the company they keep. In the case of exchange-traded funds, that company includes J.P. Morgan and similar institutional investors. If that's not good enough, I have them in my daughters' college funds and my own IRA.

4.1.3 Tax-Managed Funds

If index funds still bore you, consider the growing group of tax-managed funds. Most actively managed funds focus on raw returns, not investors' bottom lines. Fund families want strong numbers they can advertise, and appropriate numbers to compare with competitors. Since each taxpayer's situation is different, funds use pre-tax returns to measure and compare their performance.

Tax-managed funds are designed specifically for high *after-tax* return. Their goal is to marry the tax benefits of passive index funds with potentially better risk-adjusted returns of active management. They do this by avoiding turnover, matching gains with losses, selling specific shares within holdings to minimize taxable gain, and avoiding stocks that pay large dividends. Some tax-managed funds also hit sellers with an early-redemption penalty to discourage withdrawals that might force the manager to sell shares and realize gains. These funds are best suited for college savings and retirement planning outside tax-deferred accounts. They're also good for avoiding kiddie tax equal to the parents' highest rate on a child's unearned income over $1,400 per year. (See *Chapter 5.1,* "The Kiddie Tax.") Today there are nearly 50 tax-managed funds. Few of them have lengthy track records. But the category bears watching.

The ultimate tax-managed funds may be Vanguard's Tax-Managed portfolios—tax-managed versions of Vanguard's regular index funds. The Tax-Managed Growth & Income Fund tracks the S&P 500. The Tax-Managed Capital Appreciation Fund tracks the Russell 1000, a more comprehensive index of the nation's 1000 largest companies, and avoids stocks with high dividends. And the Tax-Managed Balanced portfolio invests 50% to 55% of assets in intermediate-term municipal bonds and the remaining 45% to 50% in low-dividend stocks from the Russell 1000 index. These funds start with the tax efficiency of true index funds. But the managers also use the tax-minimizing techniques above to hold down distributions. And they impose a two-tier redemption fee (2% in the first 12 months and 1% in the first five years) to discourage redemptions that could force sales and trigger capital gains.

J.P. Morgan's Tax Aware U.S. Equity Fund represents another clever twist on the tax-managed concept. This fund allows the manager to give larger shareholders ($250,000 and up) a piece of the actual portfolio when they redeem shares. This forces the departing shareholder to pay the tax, rather than distributing it to all shareholders.

4.1.4 Morningstar Tax Ratings

Morningstar is a popular mutual fund rating service, available on the internet at ***www.morningstar.com***, and in print at most libraries. A *Morningstar* rating is a single page jam-packed with information, including the fund's performance history, top holdings, a brief editorial description, and a much-misunderstood "star rating" which ranks the fund's risk-adjusted return against its peers. *Morningstar*'s tax analysis ratings are even more valuable for investors looking to make the best after-tax return:

- "Tax-adjusted return percentage" is each fund's after-tax total return. To calculate this figure, *Morningstar* "taxes" all income and capital gains distributions at the highest applicable rate and "reinvests" the remaining amount into new shares, but does not include any taxes that would result from selling the fund. The final figure doesn't represent your after-tax return. Obviously, that will depend on your own tax bracket. But it's useful whatever your tax rate to see which funds pay a greater portion of their total return in immediately taxable dividends and distributions.

- "Percentage Pre-tax Return" tells you what percentage of a fund's return consists of taxable distributions. This direct measure of tax efficiency equals the fund's after-tax return divided by its pre-tax return. A fund with a score of 100% would have no taxable distributions whatsoever.

- Finally, "Potential Capital Gains Exposure" tells you what percentage of a fund's total assets represents undistributed capital appreciation. If the fund were liquidated today, this embedded capital gain would be taxable to shareholders. As a fund's assets grow, this percentage is diluted over a larger total pool of assets. Just for kicks, here's the formula *Morningstar* uses to calculate this figure:

[Unrealized Appreciation or Depreciation + Realized Gains or Losses + (Ending NAV + Sum of Capital Gains Paid—Beginning NAV (Avg. # of shares)] -

$$\frac{\text{(Capital Gains Paid)(\# of Shares at Time of Distribution)}}{\text{Current Assets}}$$

(Don't let the formula scare you. It's like your computer. You don't have to know *how* it works. You just have to know that it *does*.)

Tax analysis ratings can vary widely, even for funds with similar objectives. The nation's five largest funds—Fidelity Magellan, Vanguard Index Trust, Investment Company of America, Washington Mutual Investors, and Fidelity Growth & Income—all qualify as large-cap blends. Yet their "Percentage Pre-tax Return" figures range from 83.7% to 92.2%. Tax-adjusted returns range from 13.82% to 17.15%. And capital gains exposure ranges from 8% to 46%.

Together, these ratings tell you which funds protect you best from taxes. They certainly aren't the place to start your search. But they're useful once you've narrowed the field.

4.1.5 Avoid High Turnover...

Fund managers generate taxable gains and losses every time they trade. It follows that managers who trade less, cost less. The turnover ratio tells you what percentage of a fund portfolio trades every year. A fund with a turnover ratio of 100, for example, turns over 100% of its value per year. Since the fund has to distribute all capital gains from this trading, higher turnover means more capital gains at tax time. Funds with high turnover also have higher expenses from research, trading, and operations. You'll find this information in the prospectus, the annual report, and sometimes the semiannual report. You'll also find it in *Morningstar*, *CDA/Wiesenberger*, and other third-party mutual fund evaluators. You'll be surprised to see that some fund managers don't actually *buy* stocks so much as they *rent* them.

Turnover isn't a direct measure of tax efficiency. The same 10% of a fund turned 10 times a year won't produce the same tax as if the entire fund had turned just once. And a fund with a 40% turnover ratio won't necessarily produce twice the tax of a fund with a 20% ratio. Turnover's effect is greatest as it commences and diminishes as it increases past 30% or so. And a manager who holds on to all of his winners may increase his fund's potential capital gains exposure (see immediately below). And some turnover can be *good*. For example, a manager who sells his losers to take advantage of tax losses saves you money even as she boosts turnover. But turnover is a useful indicator of holding period once you've narrowed your fund choices to a few final candidates.

It's also worth checking to see if a fund has just hired a new manager. This is obviously an investment consideration. A new manager might not have the proven track record of an experienced hand. But it's a tax consideration, too. When new managers take over funds, they usually clean house by selling stocks that they would not otherwise have bought and replacing them with their own favorites. This artificially gooses turnover, which boosts your eventual tax bill as a shareholder.

4.1.6 ...and Embedded Capital Gains

"Embedded capital gains" measures the percentage of a fund's NAV that consists of unrealized capital gains. If you buy into a fund with embedded capital gains, you'll eventually end up paying the tax—even if you get no economic benefit from the gain. Funds that have made money in the '90s bull market may have as much as 50% of their assets in unrealized capital gains. If those funds were to liquidate today, some shareholders could get hit with tax bills that would erase their entire gains. Of course, it's not likely that entire funds will liquidate. But if markets fall and investors panic, funds could be forced to sell stocks to meet redemptions—which would force the remaining shareholders to pay tax on those gains.

The best solution may be to buy a new fund, with no embedded capital gains. If you want to index, look for exchange-traded funds or newer funds with lower potential capital gains. You can find this information from *Morningstar*. If you want active management, look for a manager with an established track record—from another fund, perhaps, or from separate accounts.

The opposite of an embedded capital gain is a tax loss carryforward. Funds that sell losing positions in down markets can finish a year with net capital losses. This was the case with many junk bond funds in 1990; it was also the case with many small cap and emerging markets funds in 1998. But the fund doesn't distribute the loss to shareholders as it does with capital gains. Instead, the fund keeps the losses and uses them to offset future gains. The fund can carry losses forward for as many as eight years. You're most likely to find tax loss carryforwards in new funds that buy volatile asset classes.

4.2 Nine Ways to Buy and Sell Funds

Once you've chosen the right funds, it's time to build your portfolio. Here are nine strategies to buy and sell funds efficiently. Many of these strategies are the same as for individual securities. Others take advantage of mutual funds' operating structure.

4.2.1 Limit Turnover

Limiting your own turnover in your own fund portfolio works as effectively with funds as it does with individual securities. Frequent fund switching whacks your profits, just as it does when you or your fund manager trades individual stocks. And, frequent trading subjects more of your gains to punitive short-term rates, rather than long-term capital gain rates. It follows, then, that limiting your turnover lets you keep compounding money you would otherwise lose to taxes.

There are two exceptions to this rule. First, as with individual stocks, don't be afraid to walk away from a loser. And second, tax swaps may be an appropriate strategy to convert paper losses into tax savings. (See *Chapter 4.2.4*, "Tax Swaps.")

4.2.2 Keep Appropriate Records

It can be a nightmare accounting for reinvested dividends when you sell. The rules themselves are simple, but the recordkeeping is a chore. Many funds, especially income-oriented funds, pay dividends every month. If you reinvest your dividends, you'll pay different prices for each of these purchases. A fund account held for five years might include shares with 60 different prices, including ordinary income, capital gains, and fractional shares.

When you sell your shares, you pay tax on the gains on your shares. This is simple if you sell all your shares in a fund. Just add up the cost of all of your shares (including sales loads and reinvested dividends, if any), subtract that amount from the proceeds you get from the sale (minus contingent deferred sales charges, if any), and pay your tax on the difference. It gets tricky, though, if you sell just a part of your holdings. There are three ways to account for fund share costs. The method you choose can make a huge difference in your tax bill:

- The average cost method is the simplest way to calculate gains. You don't need to keep track of purchase prices or designate specific shares to sell. Just divide the number of shares into your total basis (including reinvested dividends) to determine your basis for each share sold. You can also divide your shares among those held less than a year (to be taxed as short-term gains) and those held more than a year (to be taxed as long-term gains). You can determine a separate basis for each group before figuring your gain.
- The first-in, first-out method requires you to keep track of your purchase price for each share. When you sell, you're considered to sell your oldest shares first. In rising markets, your oldest shares are usually the cheapest, generating your highest taxable gains.
- The specific share method requires you to keep track of your purchase price for each share and designate which specific shares to sell. If you've bought shares over a period of months or years at different prices, this method lets you report the lowest gain. By selling the highest-priced shares, you pay the lowest tax, since your gain will be less on the higher-priced shares.

If you buy funds in a tax-deferred account, such as an IRA, none of this recordkeeping is necessary. Every dollar you withdraw from the fund is taxed as ordinary income, unless you've made nondeductible contributions.

Finally, keeping good records will keep you from paying twice on reinvested dividends. Once you've paid tax on a dividend distribution, the amount on which you pay tax increases your basis in the fund. It can be awfully easy to forget that you've already paid tax on reinvested dividends and wind up paying tax again when you finally sell. Make sure you don't pay tax twice on your mutual fund dividends!

4.2.3 Avoid Capital Gains Distributions

All mutual funds force you to buy your neighbor's tax bill in the form of potential capital gains exposure. But buying a fund right before a capital gains distribution forces you to pay your neighbor's tax bill now. Funds accumulate capital gains throughout the year, then pay them out near the end of the year. If you own the fund on a designated date, called the ex-dividend date, you pay tax on the accumulated gains whether you actually profit from it or not. You owe the tax even if the value of the shares is less than what you paid. Where's the fun in that?

If you buy the fund just before the ex-dividend date, you'll end up paying tax on gains you don't actually earn. Let's say you buy 1,000 shares of the Gambino Growth & Income Fund for $10 apiece. The next week, the manager declares a capital gains distribution of $2 per share. You'll now own 1,000 shares worth $8,000, plus a taxable check for $2,000. This turns your pre-tax principal into taxable income. The process works the same if you direct the fund to reinvest your dividends. Now, instead of owning 1,000 shares at $8.00 each, plus a $2,000 taxable dividend check, you'll own 1,250 shares at $8 each, and you'll still owe tax on your 250 "new" shares.

4.2.4 Tax Swaps

A tax swap is when you sell an investment at a loss, then replace it with a similar or identical investment. Mutual funds that invest in similar assets let you sell a poor performer and replace it with a different family's fund. Your portfolio looks the same, but you realize a loss to offset gains or even ordinary income. Mutual fund tax swaps let you realize capital losses while keeping the same sort of fund.

Why not just buy back the same fund? The wash sale rule says that if you sell an investment at a loss, then buy it back within 31 days before or after the original sale date, your loss is disallowed as a wash sale. This rule limits your chance to net out capital gains with unrealized losses. But individual mutual funds are considered unique securities. This is true even for two funds that invest in similar assets. If you sell one family's growth fund to buy another family's fund, you'll beat the wash sale rule even if both funds' portfolios are exactly the same.

The strategy, then, is to find another fund with the same investment objective and similar holdings as your current fund. After you sell your current fund at a loss, transfer your money into the new fund. You can use the loss to wipe out an equal amount of capital gains, or up to $3,000 of ordinary income.

Let's say that you buy the Gambino Emerging Markets fund for $10,000. The Mexican peso collapses and your fund is now worth $7,000. You'd like to realize the loss to shelter your $3,000 dividend income from the Gambino Bond Fund. But, you'd also like to stay invested in emerging markets. What do you do? Consider selling the Gambino Emerging Markets Fund and buying the Lucchese Emerging Markets Fund. You realize a $3,000 capital loss to offset your capital gain, and stay invested in your chosen market.

This strategy is even more useful for index funds and commodity fund categories like Treasury bond funds, where most fund families' portfolios are similar. It's also useful for funds held less than a year, since short-term capital gains are taxed at ordinary income rates. But be careful with this strategy. Don't pay unnecessary loads or higher expense ratios for the sake of short-term tax savings.

4.2.5 Write Off Sales Loads

If you buy a fund through a broker, you'll pay some sort of commission, or load, for the broker's service. There are three main flavors of load. Front-end loads are traditional sales commissions paid up front to acquire shares. Back-end loads, or contingent deferred sales charges, are similar to the penalty on early withdrawals for bank CDs, for shares redeemed within the first few years of ownership. Finally, level loads are ongoing asset management fees of up to 1% per year similar to the management fee you'd pay to a private money manager.

Here's a strategy to write off front-end loads. Remember, once you've paid your load, you're free to switch funds within the family at no extra charge. If you buy into a family, then immediately switch into another fund, you'll show a short-term capital loss equal to the load. You can use the loss to offset capital gains or up to $3,000 of ordinary income. For example, if your broker recommends the Gambino Emerging Markets Fund, first buy shares in the Gambino Equity Fund (or any fund with the same sales load), then immediately transfer your funds into the emerging markets fund. (This strategy works only in taxable accounts, not IRAs.)

When you finally sell your shares, your basis for figuring gain or loss will be lower than if you hadn't used this strategy. Still, the extra gain you delay until your sale will be taxed at lower long-term gain rates (assuming you keep the shares longer than a year), while your up-front loss will offset ordinary income and short-term gains. Your savings up front are greater than the extra tax at the end. The net result of the strategy is to convert an amount equal to your load from ordinary income into capital gains.

4.2.6 Dividends to Capital Gains

It's clearly a rookie mistake to buy a fund just before the ex-dividend date. But you can use this same structural quirk to *avoid* tax on shares you plan to sell. This strategy also takes advantage of the ex-dividend date to convert ordinary income into capital gains. It's actually the reverse of avoiding purchases near year-end.

When a mutual fund distributes a dividend, the price of each share falls by the amount distributed as a dividend. That dividend is then taxed as ordinary income or capital gain. If you're ready to sell shares you've held for more than a year, and you sell when the shares are fat right before a dividend, you'll pay capital gains tax on the portion of the value that might otherwise soon be distributed as an income dividend. This strategy makes little difference with capital gains dividends that are taxed as long-term capital gains already. But you can squeeze out some extra tax savings by selling future income dividends as capital gains. (This can also help with year-end planning. If you buy shares in a high-tax year, use this strategy to cut that year's income.)

4.2.7 Beware Checkwriting…

Many short-term bond funds come with a checkbook that lets you redeem shares merely by writing a check. The fund company then pays the recipient of the check directly. This is a wonderful convenience. But, each time you write a check, you're selling shares, with different holding periods and cost bases. And you can't specify which shares to sell. Your fund's prospectus will tell you which shares you can expect to be liquidated. (This isn't a problem with money market funds, which don't generate capital gains when you redeem shares.) This doesn't mean you should throw away the checkbook. Just be aware of the bookkeeping hassles it creates.

4.2.8 ...Systematic Withdrawals...

A systematic withdrawal plan pays you a specified dollar amount from your fund at a specified period—generally, monthly or quarterly. The fund pays out accumulated income first, then sells shares if accumulated income isn't enough to pay the entire distribution. Systematic withdrawal plans are an excellent alternative to annuitization for investors who need steady, predictable income from their holdings.

Systematic withdrawal plans let you manage your portfolio for total return and still draw a regular income. Many investors mistakenly believe they should manage for income and never touch principal. But if you invest for income, you give up much of the potential long-term growth you need to protect against inflation. A systematic withdrawal plan first pays out your income you earn. If that's not enough, it makes up the difference with capital gains and principal.

The problem, of course, is that, like checkwriting, systematic withdrawal plans force you to sell shares at different times and different prices. This can make bookkeeping hard. If you confine your systematic withdrawals to tax-deferred accounts, you'll avoid a lot of paperwork.

4.2.9 ...and Rebalancing

Portfolio rebalancing simply means maintaining your target asset allocation. Let's say you choose to keep $50,000 in stocks and $50,000 in bonds. At the end of your first year, your stocks may be worth $55,000 and your bonds $53,000. Rebalancing would require you to sell $1,000 of stocks and invest the proceeds in bonds to maintain your 50-50 split. If you *don't* rebalance, your asset allocation drifts away from your target.

Portfolio rebalancing may not boost your return. If high return is your goal, then choose the invest-ment that's likely to pay the highest return over time, and dive on in. But, by ensuring that your assets don't become concentrated in volatile sectors, it does help limit your risk. And, it forces you to buy low—when one asset class lags the rest of your portfolio—and sell high, when another races ahead.

The problem, as you've already guessed, is that rebalancing forces you to recognize capital gains. This generates tax bills—and possible transaction costs, too. There are two solutions. First, replenish your laggards with new money. Second, confine rebalancing to your tax-deferred accounts. Many retirement plan and variable annuities offer automatic rebalancing services, perhaps quarterly or annually.

4.3   Closed-End Funds

Closed-end funds are different from their more popular open-ended cousins. Closed-end funds issue fixed numbers of shares to an original group of investors. Then, instead of redeeming shares directly from investors, the fund trades on an open market such as the New York Stock Exchange. If you want to sell your shares, you have to find another investor willing to buy them—and you may not get the net asset value (NAV) of the fund's underlying portfolio.

In fact, closed-end funds hardly ever trade at the net asset value of their underlying holdings. Closed-end fund fans argue that this offers bargain opportunities—"stocks at a discount." A share that costs you $20 might represent $21 worth of underlying holdings. Buy the fund at a discount, and wait for the discount to narrow, or even disappear. This way, you profit even if the portfolio's NAV stays flat. But I'm not a fan of this argument. The problem is that when you buy a closed-end fund, you're not just buying a portfolio of stocks, you're also obligating yourself to pay the fund's management fee. This isn't burdensome with the new breed of inexpensive exchange-traded funds. But it can be a real burden with closed-end fund fees topping one and in some cases even two percent per year. Why should you ever pay $21, plus a management fee, for a portfolio that you could assemble for $21 without the fee? Closed-end funds *should* trade at a discount, equal to the discounted present value of the sum of future management fees. Many closed-end fund fans just flat-out miss this structural flaw.

The worst offense is buying a closed-end fund at its initial public offering. You'll pay a hefty commission, plus ongoing management fees, for a fund that's doomed to trade at an immediate discount once investors on the secondary market can buy without the initial commission. Never buy a closed-end fun at its initial public offering.

Closed-end funds are taxed like their opened-end cousins. Income dividends are taxed immediately as ordinary income, just like with open-end funds. When you sell your shares you'll owe capital gains tax on the profits from the sale. However, since there are no reinvested dividends, closed-end funds avoid the confusion open-ended funds cause with reinvested dividends.

America's most famous investor, the legendary Warren Buffet, runs what qualifies as a closed-end fund. His company, Berkshire-Hathaway, is a former textile mill with stock holdings in some of America's greatest companies: Coca-Cola, GEICO, The Washington Post Company, and even NetJets, a corporate aircraft fractional-ownership program. These holdings themselves are a viable alternative to closed-end funds. The shares have above $80,000 each, and carry a "premium" of up to 50% above NAV. (Buffet himself is worth north of $30 billion.) The company is wonderfully tax-efficient; it pays no dividend, so shareholders pay no tax until they sell their shares.

Finally, there is a small group of closed-end funds that have issued preferred shares paying a guaranteed income taxed partially as capital gains. They do this by distributing long-term gains to the preferred shareholders and reserving the bulk of ordinary income dividends for common shareholders. The long-term capital gain portion of the dividend is taxed at your long-term capital gains rate rather than your ordinary income rate.

Of course, if fund income isn't enough to cover preferred yields, the funds' common shareholders lose. These preferred shares might be an attractive option for investors seeking high current income. (Currently, closed-end funds paying preferred dividends include the Gabelli Global Multimedia Trust, the Royce OTC Micro-Cap Trust, and the Royce Value Trust.

4.4   Unit Investment Trusts

Unit investment trusts (UITs), are unmanaged portfolios assembled by a broker and sold to investors. UITs have traditionally bought and held municipal bonds. However, equity trusts are now becoming more popular. You pay a fee to the sponsor and a commission to the broker. UITs are more efficient than actively managed funds because there's no turnover. That means your gains are deferred until you sell the entire package. But higher fees may erase the tax savings.

Several brokerage houses have joined together to offer UITs using the "dogs of the Dow[sm]" strategy. (See *Chapter 3.1.3*, "The Dogs of the Dow.") The trust buys the 10 highest-yielding stocks of the Dow Jones Industrial Average and holds them for a year and a day. You can redeem your shares or reinvest them in a new trust. This is an inexpensive way to invest small amounts into the strategy. But it's even less efficient that buying the stocks directly. That's because the UIT forces you to pay tax on all of the gains in the trust, even those on stocks that you would carry over to another year. If you buy these UITs, do it in your IRA. Otherwise, the tax you pay erases the benefit of the strategy.

4.5 Hedge Funds

Hedge funds, along with their cousins, venture capital funds and buy-out funds, are private investment partnerships. These are the glamorous and secretive celebrities of the managed money world. Managers like George Soros, manager of the Quantum Fund, and John Meriwether, ringmaster of the ill-fated Long-Term Capital Management, capture headlines and move markets. They also catch the blame when markets fall and currencies collapse. The funds themselves usually accept contributions of $1 million and up. The most coveted funds operating offshore or require as much as $10 million to join. Some funds let groups of smaller investors pool their money into partnerships of their own to reach these minimums. Hedge funds are less liquid than publicly traded mutual funds. Usually, there's just one annual chance to redeem your investment. Managers can pay out over a period of time or even suspend redemptions entirely to protect remaining partners. And, you can't track your investment in the paper like you can with a publicly traded fund. Despite these disadvantages, hedge funds are estimated to manage upwards of $300 billion.

Hedge funds use sophisticated strategies like options, futures, short sales, and arbitrage. Despite the implication that hedge funds aim primarily to reduce risk, many hedge funds have become high-octane speculators. These cowboys don't just try to beat the market. They want to kick its ass. And they're expensive: a typical fee is 1% of assets, *plus* 20% of profits. To put a little perspective on how those fees add up, consider this. None of the *Forbes* 400 richest Americans made their fortune *investing* in hedge funds. But several, including Soros (net worth $4 billion) and Julian Robertson, manager of the Tiger Fund (net worth $1.7 billion), made their money *running* them.

Hedge funds trade furiously; turnover is high. So taxes are naturally high. You'll have to decide for yourself if the gains, after taxes and fees, justify the risk and illiquidity. (Nashville-based Van Hedge Fund Advisors has calculated that a group of nearly 3,000 domestic and offshore hedge funds significantly underperformed the S&P 500 from January 1, 1993 through October 31, 1998.) But there are a tax breaks if you choose to play this game:

- You can buy a hedge fund "swap" or "option" from an investment bank. You give your money to the bank in exchange for the swap, and the bank buys the fund and pays you the return. Instead of paying short-term gains on the actual fund itself, you pay long-term gains on the swap or option the bank creates. These can require minimums of $5 million or more. (The 1999 budget bill, signed by President Clinton on December 17, 1999, eliminates this loophole for contracts entered into after that date.)
- You can buy private-placement variable life insurance that invests in hedge funds. These also require super-high minimum investments.
- You can buy retail mutual funds marketed as hedge funds for the masses. Market neutral funds hold both long and short positions in an attempt to eliminate market risk. "Bear" funds use options and other derivatives to profit when the market falls. Most investors who use bear funds hold them briefly to profit from short-term drops. Both of these fund categories are best suited for your tax-deferred accounts.
- Venture capital investors can buy publicly traded stocks that invest much like venture capital partnerships. Hold these shares in tax-deferred accounts to avoid current taxes.

4.6 Separate Accounts

Mutual funds, UITs, and hedge funds offer professional investment management for all ranges of investors. But they might not be your best money management choice. Separate account managers take your money and customize a portfolio especially for you. They require higher minimum investments. But they give you more service, more handholding, and far more control over your tax bill than their publicly-traded mutual fund cousins.

When you buy a mutual fund, UIT, or hedge fund, you choose a money manager, then give them your money in exchange for a piece of a single security—the fund itself. (You can hold the security with the fund company, or you can hold it in a brokerage account.) Your manager directs the fund, and the fund itself owns the underlying investments. You can track the fund's daily closing price in the newspaper or on the Internet. Managers report specific holdings semiannually.

When you open a separate account, you choose a money manager, then give them your money to establish a separate account of your own. (Typically, you'll establish an account in your own name with a discount broker like Schwab or Waterhouse.) Your manager runs the money, while you actually own the underlying investments. You can track your holdings as often as you like in the newspaper or the Internet. This may seem like a subtle difference. But it offers important advantages:

- Separate accounts let your manager invest specifically for taxable or tax-deferred accounts. Mutual funds accept both taxable and tax-deferred money, and most manage solely for pre-tax returns.
- Separate accounts for taxable investors give you more control over your holdings than mutual funds, UITs, and hedge funds. You can direct your manager to avoid tobacco stocks, casinos, and the like.
- Separate accounts can serve as "completion funds" to round out large holdings in a single company or industry. If you've retired from Procter & Gamble with a big block of their stock, the last thing you need is more P&G stock. Separate accounts let you avoid P&G specifically, or the entire consumer goods sector, while exposing you to technology, finance, utilities, and other sectors.

- Separate accounts don't carry embedded capital gains like mutual funds. The average mutual fund carries an embedded gain of about 20%. Separate accounts establish separate cost bases and holding periods for each security you buy.

- Separate accounts give you far more control over after-tax returns than funds. You can choose tax-managed accounts that avoid turnover, match gains and losses, and sell high-cost basis stock first. You can direct your manager to realize gains or losses on your schedule, to manage your tax liability. Separate accounts insulate you from other investors. If the market tanks, you don't have to worry about other investors bailing ship, forcing the manager to sell stocks and, in turn, forcing you to pay tax on a commingled fund's gains.

- Separate accounts offer declining fees as assets rise. In contrast, funds charge you the same fee on expense on every dollar under management.

- Separate accounts let you carve out a specific portion of your holdings to sell or give to charity.

- Many separate account managers will open an account with securities. This is important because you don't have to liquidate existing holdings and pay immediate tax on your gains in order to participate.

- If your manager is a bust, you can transfer your assets to another manager without liquidating holdings and recognizing capital gains. With mutual funds, in contrast, you have to sell your shares in the dog and pay all your taxes before giving the money to the new manager.

There are several ways to hire separate account managers:

- You can find a manager yourself. This is the least expensive path. But it obviously involves the most work—both to select your manager and to monitor their performance against competitors and benchmarks. Separate account managers include local "boutiques," regional and national powerhouses with billions under management, bank trust departments, and specialized trust companies with widely ranging account minimums, fees, and track records.

- You can hire a consultant to find a manager. This lets you access more managers than you can comfortably research yourself.
- Finally, you can open a "wrap account" for an entire bundle of investment management services. These accounts include financial planning, investment management, performance reporting, trading commissions, and account maintenance fees. Typical participants may include a broker, who provides financial planning services, a "third-party asset management provider," or consultant, who chooses a specific money manager from a pre-approved list, and finally the money manager itself. The best programs include dozens of managers and investment styles. Extra services might include conference calls and road shows to meet the manager. These accounts open the door to money managers and investment styles that you might not otherwise be able to afford. For example, one manager I've recommended to my own clients requires a $5 million portfolio to establish a tax-aware portfolio directly—but lowers that minimum to just $100,000 for clients of a specific third-party asset management consultant.

Wrap accounts have historically cost more than funds. Published fees generally began at 3%, although most brokers and financial planners can discount these rates. But wrap accounts fees have become more competitive with funds. And they're far better than variable annuities for most investors who qualify! If your portfolio is large enough to qualify, take a look at the various separate account programs available through your full-service broker or financial planner.

Separate account fees are deductible as an investment expense, up to the amount of investment income, subject to the 2% floor on miscellaneous itemized deductions. You can also write off account costs, such as IRA custodial fees. Include commissions to buy and sell individual securities in your adjusted cost basis and sales prices for figuring gains and losses on sales.

4.7   "Basket" Portfolios

Basket portfolios are the newest wrinkle in managed money, and are entirely a creature of the Internet. These services let you buy a "basket" of up to 50 shares that you own individually, generally for a set fee per month. (Smaller investors may wind up with fractional shares that they trade through the basket sponsor. Internet and computer cost efficiencies make this sort of trading affordable.) This individual ownership lets you manage your taxes by offsetting winners and losers and choosing when to take your gains. Basket sponsors offer asset allocation and portfolio planning tools in addition to assembling the baskets. Some services let you trade entire baskets at specific times of day, while others let you buy and sell throughout the day.

Basket portfolio fees today range from $20 to $30 per month, depending on the number of baskets you buy. This means that an investor with $10,000 would pay a management fee of 3.6%; while an investor with $100,000 would pay 0.36%. Be sure to compare these fees with managed money alternatives before investing.

Basket portfolio sponsors have a long and distinguished history, dating back to the previous millennium-1999. This form of ownership is so new that you're best off consulting individual sponsors for more information. As of this writing, you can find basket portfolio sponsors at *www.foliofn.com, www.netfolio.com, www.personalfund.com*, and *www.unx.com*, among others. By the time you read these words, there may be dozens more of these services available, including programs sponsored by progressive investment firms such as E*Trade and Charles Schwab.

Chapter 5

Family Tax Planning

Shifting investments and investment income to lower-bracket taxpayers—usually your kids, but also parents or other relatives—is a classic tool for cutting income tax. These strategies have the extra advantage of cutting estate taxes at your death. The more income-producing investments you transfer out of your estate, the lower that last tax bill will be. Since the federal estate tax ranges up to 55%, these are some of the most powerful tax strategies around.

The Tax Reform Act of 1986 clamped down on income shifting by imposing a kiddie tax equal to the parents' highest rate on unearned income over $1,400 (indexed for inflation) for children under age 14. The tax applies to trust fund distributions, custodial accounts, and even S corporation and partnership income. But shifting income still remains a valuable strategy for cutting your own tax while transferring family assets to the next generation.

Most of these strategies involve some sort of gift to a family member. So, before we look at specific family gift strategies, we need to look at the general rules surrounding gifts and gift taxes. The gift tax is actually an element of the unified gift and estate tax system, which taxes on your ability to transfer assets. There's never any tax due on the part of the recipient; gifts and inheritances are *not* taxable income. (Some states levy an inheritance tax on your right to receive assets.)

There is a gift tax annual exclusion of $10,000 per donor, per recipient. This means that you can give $10,000 per year to as many people as you want without paying gift tax. If your spouse joins you, you can give $20,000 split gifts to as many people as you want. If you and your spouse make split gifts, you'll need to file IRS *Form 709*; however, there will be no tax due and no effect on your unified credit.

If your gifts to any person top $10,000 in a year, you'll owe gift tax on the amount over $10,000. However, you don't actually pay tax until your combined taxable gifts exceed the gift/estate tax unified credit exemption equivalent. This amount is $650,000 for 1999, and is scheduled to rise to $1 million by 2007. Thus, the amount of any taxable gift above $10,000 per year to an individual recipient will eat away at the amount you can leave to your heirs without paying estate tax. Once you've exhausted your credit, you start paying tax. Use *Form 709* to report taxable gifts and calculate the tax.

These family gifting strategies carry one significant disadvantage. The lucky recipient takes the property with a carryover basis equal to your own at the time of the gift. That means there's no chance to avoid tax on accumulated gains through a stepped-up basis at your death. You'll need to consider whether current tax savings outweigh the loss of the stepped-up basis. Some gifting strategies may save more in estate tax than they cost in income tax, justifying the sacrifice. You can also consider giving assets that provide most of their total return in taxable income, such as bonds, rather than investments that provide long-term capital gains, such as real estate and stocks.

5.1   The Kiddie Tax

Shifting income to your lower-bracket kids is an obvious strategy. So, Congress imposes a "kiddie tax" equal to your highest marginal rate on your kids' investment income over $1,400 per year. The purpose is simply to keep you from shifting income to children under age 14. Here's how it works:

- If your child has less than $700 of total income, there's no need to file a return.
- If the child has investment income, file a return once your child's total income tops $700.
- If the child has earned income but no investment income, file a return once your child's earned income tops $4,150.
- The kiddie tax kicks in once your child's net investment income tops $1,400. (If your child itemizes deductions and has more than $700 in deductible investment expenses, the floor is $700 plus the deductible investment expenses.)
- To determine the actual kiddie tax, first determine your own tax. Then, determine how much your children's income subject to the tax increases your tax. Finally, allocate the extra tax to each child in proportion to each child's income subject to the tax.
- Determine the tax on *Form 8615*. You can attach it to the child's return or to your own.
- If you're married filing separately, use the larger separate income to determine the kiddie tax. If you're divorced, use the income of the parent with custody for the greatest part of the year.
- Your child's income doesn't increase your AGI for purposes of figuring limits on deductions or credits. For example, your child's income won't prevent you from contributing to an IRA.

If your children's income is solely from interest and dividends, you can report it all on your own return with *Form 8814*. You'll pay $97.50 (15% of the child's first $700) plus 15% of the child's income over $700, plus whatever kiddie tax is due. This saves you the trouble of filing your child's own return. However, this *will* increase your own AGI for purposes of figuring limits on deductions or credits. Be sure you aren't raising your own tax to save on paperwork.

Just how much can you save by putting investments in your child's name? You can actually invest a substantial amount of money without cracking that $1,400 limit—as much as you want if it doesn't pay a dividend. A stock fund paying a 2% dividend can grow to $65,000 before the income distribution tops $1,400. The tax on that $1,400 will be just $97.50. If you're in the 28% bracket, you'd pay $364; in the 39.6% bracket you'd pay $514.80.

Here are two strategies to avoid generating unearned income in your child's name:

- Buy U.S. Savings Bonds that matures after your child turns 14.
- Buy municipal bonds—especially deep-discount municipal zeroes—in your child's name.

5.1.1 Custodial Accounts

Children under the age of majority can't hold investment property in their own name. Some sort of trust or custodial account is necessary. Custodial accounts are the most common because they require less paperwork (and no legal fees!) to establish. Each state has a Uniform Gifts to Minors (UGMA) or Uniform Transfers to Minors (UTMA) statute governing these accounts. Here's how they work:

- First, you establish an account with an adult as custodian to hold the investments for the benefit of the beneficiary child.
- You can use funds from the account for the benefit of the child. But, you can't use the child's funds to cover your parental responsibilities.
- Income from the account is reported under the child's Social Security number and taxed under the rules above.

If you apply for college financial aid, your child's school will expect the child to use a greater percentage of that money for tuition than if you had held the funds yourself. If you expect to pay for college without applying for financial aid, this makes no difference. But if you know that you and your child will be applying for help, be aware that saving money in your child's name will hurt your chances.

When the child reaches majority, usually at age 21, the assets in the account revert to the child alone. But there are safety valves if your kids are about to blow the money on motorcycles and drugs. For example, you can use funds to buy a minority interest in your own house. Or you can contribute to a family limited partnership or other vehicle that limits their control.

5.1.2 Minors' Trusts

If you'd rather not hand over control of your kids' money at age 21, you can establish a trust to hold their assets. Trusts do carry some special restrictions that make them less useful than you might expect:

- You can't use trust funds to pay for your own parental obligations. That means you can't use trust assets for housing, support, medical care, and the like. One court has even ruled that parents who can afford it have the obligation to pay for their kids' college.
- The trust will owe tax on any income that you as trustee don't distribute to the beneficiaries. That may not sound like such a burden—after all, your kids owe tax on their custodial account earnings, right? The problem is that trust tax brackets rise far faster than for individuals: 15% on the first $1,750; 28% on the next $2,300; 31% on the next $2,150; 36% on the next $2,250, and 39.6% on anything above $8,450. The solution is to invest trust assets so that they don't generate current income.

5.2 College Savings Strategies

College funding is most families' financial bogeyman. Once the baby arrives, the clock starts ticking. And college costs climb faster than inflation, each and every year. We tell ourselves that someday, it has to stop. But it never does. In early 1999, I calculated how much it would cost to send my daughters, Molly, age 7, and Mary Claire, age 2, to my alma mater, Hamilton. If I can do it without paying taxes, it will cost just $234.15—per *week*. Now you know why I write about taxes.

Here are six tax-advantaged college savings strategies to consider. Some are more effective than others. Unfortunately, you can't just look at college savings strategies. If you anticipate applying for financial aid, you'll need to consider how they intersect with financial aid strategies. You can save taxes with custodial accounts and Education IRAs; however, these may blow your child's chance to qualify for grants and loans.

5.2.1 Education IRAs

Education IRAs are tax-deferred college savings accounts that let you invest wherever you see fit. The concept is sound, and we discuss them first because they seem like such an obvious choice. But the Education IRAs are weak and don't deliver real benefit. Here's how they work:

- Each child can accept up to $500 per year from donors with AGIs up to $110,000 ($160,000 for joint filers).
- The child can't accept contributions in a year in which he or she receives a contribution to a qualified state tuition program.
- When the child reaches college, you can withdraw as much as necessary to pay the child's college costs, including room and board. These

withdrawals are tax-free. If you take out more than the child's college costs, your child will pay tax at his or her rate on whatever portion of the IRA's earnings equal the percentage of the withdrawal used for college costs.

- If the child dies, the account balance must be distributed to his or her estate within 30 days of his or her death.
- If the child doesn't use the money by his or her 30th birthday, the funds have to be distributed and taxed, along with a 10% penalty, or rolled into another family member's Education IRA.

They *sound* like a great deal. But the $500 annual contribution limit—just $9,000 through age 18—keeps you from accumulating enough to make a difference. Compounding $500 per year at 10.5% grows to just $26,482 after 18 years. That's not pocket change—but it isn't likely to cover more than a semester at the nation's elite universities. You can't claim the new Hope Scholarship or Lifetime Learning tax credits for a student in a year when you take money from that student's Education IRA. And currently, it's not clear how Education IRA balances will affect financial aid formulas. There hasn't been a great demand for these accounts, and many investment providers don't even offer them.

5.2.2 Prepaid Tuition Programs

Prepaid tuition programs, or "Section 529 plans," are tax-advantaged college savings plans administered by the states. These are far better programs than education IRAs. Some of them guarantee you a future unit of tuition—a credit hour, a course, or even an entire year—at today's price. Others invest in a selection of mutual funds, without guaranteeing a final value. The real benefit is the higher contribution limit. In addition, there's no conflict with the Hope Scholarship or Lifetime Learning tax credit, as there is with the Education IRA. Here are the rules:

- Your earnings grow tax-deferred until you withdraw them to pay college costs.
- Your withdrawals are treated first as a return of your original investment, with no tax due until your total withdrawals top your total investment in the program.
- Withdrawals exceeding the investment in the program are taxed to your child at his or her lower rate. You pay tax only if you get a refund exceeding your initial investment.
- Contributions are considered complete gifts for gift tax purposes. Parents or grandparents can put up to $10,000 per year into the program and owe no gift tax. A special rule lets you give up to $50,000 in a single year ($100,000 for couples) so long as you make no further contribution for the next four years.

You don't have to choose your own state's program. And the new generation of mutual fund programs, such as Maine's NextGen College Investing Program^{sm}, (Merrill Lynch), Colorado's Scholars Choice (Citigroup), and New Hampshire's UNIQUE College Investing Plan (Fidelity Investments) may be the best college savings strategy available. The fund managers invest your savings, and the program managers adjust the portfolio mix as your child approaches college—all tax-free. For more information on these programs, consult the National Association of State Treasurers web sites at *www.collegesavings.org*. You'll find links to web sites, e-mail addresses, and toll-free numbers for every plan across the country.

5.2.3 Savings Bonds

Series EE and Series I U.S. Savings Bond income may be partially or fully tax-free if you redeem them to pay college costs. (For more information, see *Chapter 2.2.4*, "Savings Bonds.") Savings Bonds won't generate the income you need to keep up with college costs. However, they can be a good parking place in anticipation that you'll use it soon. You have to own the bonds in your own name, not your child's. That means you can't use this strategy in a custodial account.

5.2.4 Custodial Accounts

As we've already seen, you can use custodial accounts to cut tax on investments in your child's name. However, custodial accounts have a strong drawback when you use them to save for college. If you apply for financial aid, the college will expect you to use a larger percentage of the assets in your child's account for tuition than if the assets were held elsewhere. This will hurt your child's eligibility for financial aid.

5.2.5 Life Insurance

Cash value life insurance can be a powerful college savings tool. You can tap your earnings tax-free through loans and basis withdrawals. And, if you're not around to pay the bill yourself, the insurance does it for you. Life insurance can be expensive. However, if you have school-age children, you probably need the coverage. But keep these points in mind. First, life insurance has long surrender periods. If you withdraw money too soon, you may face steep surrender periods. The best time to buy a policy is when the child is born—precisely when money is tightest, but also when the need is the greatest. Second, you have to keep the policy in force in order to avoid paying tax on any withdrawals exceeding your basis in the contract—the total premiums you have paid.

5.2.6 Retirement Accounts

There are two ways to use your retirement accounts to pay for tuition with tax-advantaged dollars. These may be appropriate if you can tap them without jeopardizing your own retirement security. Here's how they work:

- You can withdraw an unlimited amount of money from your ordinary IRA to pay college costs. You'll owe regular tax on the withdrawal, but not the usual 10% penalty for withdrawals before age 59½.
- You can withdraw money from a Roth IRA tax-free if you meet the age and holding-period requirements. You can withdraw your contributions tax-free even if you don't meet the age and holding-period requirements for tax-free income.

5.3 Strategies for Adult Children

Once your children outgrow the kiddie tax, your family planning strategies grow. And, as the kids mature, you'll get a better idea how well they handle money. If you find yourself with the next Menendez brothers, that may count more than taxes.

5.3.1 Trusts

There are a wide variety of trusts you can use to transfer assets and cut your tax. Most of these are established for estate-planning purposes. But, there can be income tax benefits, too.

- You can use incentive trusts to reward heirs for things like graduating from college. But be careful. Playboy Tommy Manville, heir to the Johns-Manville fortune, inherited a trust giving him a $250,000 payout when he married. Tommy married 13 times, proving you can be rich and still marry for money.
- Grantor-retained annuitrusts (GRATs) and grantor-retained unitrusts (GRUTs) work like charitable remainder trusts except that you give the remainder interest to a family beneficiary instead of a charity. Naturally, there's no charitable deduction. But it transfers the assets and future appreciation out of your estate.
- "Defective" grantor trust are drafted so they *fail* the grantor trust requirements. This means that you, and not the beneficiaries, owe tax on the trust income. The twist here is that the tax you pay is not counted as a gift for gift tax purposes. This lets you increase your gifts to the trust beneficiaries by the tax you pay—on top of the gift or principal. These are excellent choices for large gifts exceeding the estate/gift tax unified credit.
- See *Chapter 7.3* for information on irrevocable life insurance trusts.

5.3.2 Loans

Low-interest loans are a way to give investment capital to lower-bracket family members. The borrower can then invest the loan proceeds and earn income above the loan interest to be taxed at their lower rate. You have to charge a reasonable rate of interest, or the IRS will impute a reasonable rate and tax the difference as a gift to the recipient.

5.3.3 Family Limited Partnerships

Family limited partnerships, or FLPs, have become a popular tax-planning and asset protection tool. You form a limited partnership with yourself and perhaps other family members as general partner. Next, you transfer family assets into the partnership. There's no tax consequence with this transfer. You can then give limited partnership interests to family members. These gifts generally qualify as complete gifts for gift tax exclusion purposes. Your general partnership interest assures your continued control over partnership assets. Yet their limited partnership interests means that they pay tax on their share of partnership income at their presumably lower rates. This makes a FLP an effective tool to shift taxes to lower-bracket family members without giving up control over assets. It's even more useful for assets such as real estate or a business that you can't simply divide without sacrificing control.

You can also take a gift and estate tax valuation discount reflecting the lack of marketability. If you give your son $10,000 worth of stock, he can turn around and sell it tomorrow. If you give him a 10% limited partnership share in a partnership owning $100,000 worth of stock, he's stuck. Although he'll owe tax on the income from the stock, his inability to sell his interest makes his share of the partnership less valuable than the underlying stock. Valuation discounts of up to 40% aren't uncommon. This lets you transfer up to $16,666 worth of assets to a single recipient while remaining within the $10,000 annual gift tax exclusion. This can be an effective tool for transferring appreciation out of your estate. But remember, when your heirs pull their property out of the partnership, they'll take it with the same basis as when it was transferred into the FLP. You'll have to consider whether the estate tax savings outweigh the loss of stepped-up basis at your death.

Transferring assets to a FLP also places them out of your creditors' reach. They can't reach inside the partnership to seize the underlying assets. The best they usually get is a charging order entitling them to income distributions. However, they will then owe tax on that income—even if you as the general partner don't actually distribute it. This makes FLPs even more popular with doctors, attorneys, and S&L swindlers. You can't use a FLP to shield assets from present creditors—those whom you know or should know have a present claim against you. If you try, the transfer can be voided as a fraudulent conveyance. But you can use a FLP to protect yourself from future creditors. (I tell my doctor clients that if they hear the nurse say "whoops!" it's too late.)

5.3.4 Private Annuities

A private annuity can pay you tax-advantaged income today, transfer assets to your heirs, and cut your estate tax. It combines the tax advantages of an immediate annuity and an installment sale to hold down tax on your lifetime income. It also removes the value of the asset, plus any future appreciation, from your estate. With a private annuity, you sell part or all of an asset, such as real estate or a family business, to your heirs in exchange for a lifetime annuity income. The income is determined according to annuity valuation factors and the applicable federal rate in effect at the time of the sale. Part of your income will consist of nontaxable return of principal, taxed under the rules for immediate annuities. Another part will consist of capital gain, taxed under the rules for installment sales. The final part consists of interest income from the installment sale. And, since the income stops at your death, the arrangement leaves nothing to be taxed in your estate.

Let's say you own a sporting goods store. You're a man, age 65, with a life expectancy of 15 years. The business has a basis of $100,000 and a fair market value of $200,000. And the applicable federal rate is 9%. You can sell the business to your child in exchange for a lifetime income of $2,028.53 per month, which represents a generous 12.17% income. The first $555.55 of each month's payment will be considered a tax-free return of your $100,000 basis under the rules governing immediate annuities. The next $555.55 will be taxed as capital gain under the rules governing installment sales. The final $917.43 is taxable as interest. (After 180 payments, when you've recovered your $100,000 basis and paid tax on your $100,000 gain, the entire payment will be taxed as income.) At your death, the income stops and there's nothing left in your estate. If you use part of the annuity income to fund an irrevocable life insurance trust, you can replace the entire $200,000 for your heirs, with no income or estate taxes at all.

If, on the other hand, you sell the business outright, you'll owe tax on your $100,000 capital gain at the time of the sale. You'll also owe estate tax on whatever part of the proceeds are leftover at your death.

Here are some more points to consider:

- You can draft the annuity to provide for a life income or a joint income. If you keep a period-certain guarantee, the value of that guarantee is taxable in your estate.
- You can adjust the payout for terminal illness or some other factor affecting your life expectancy.
- If you're worried about the person paying the income dying before they fulfilling their obligation to you, you can informally buy insurance on their life. However, you can't keep a security interest in the payments or the value of that interest will revert back to your estate.

Chapter 6

Retirement Plans

Retirement plans, including employer-sponsored plans, self-employed plans, and IRAs, are the first place to turn for tax-deferred investing. That's because most contributions give you an up-front deduction as well as tax-deferred growth. Most retirement plan balances are also protected from creditors, either by federal pension law in the case of qualified plans or state law in the case of IRAs. These are the same protections that let O.J. Simpson spend his life on the golf course in the face of a multi-million dollar judgment after butchering his ex-wife and her innocent friend.

6.1   Tax-Deferred Compounding

Albert Einstein is said to have called tax-deferred compounding the eighth wonder of the world. You probably already know about the power of compound interest: you earn interest on your original principal, plus interest on the interest. In a taxable account, you pay tax on the interest each year, and lose a little piece of your earnings. This leaves less to compound and slows your growth on your investment. But in a tax-deferred account, you don't pay tax until you take out your money. With tax-deferred compounding, you earn interest on your principal, interest on the interest, and interest on the tax savings.

Tax-deferred accounts let you throw out the rules we learned about turnover. Since there's no tax on earnings—only withdrawals—there's no need to worry about the percentage of gains from long-term capital gains, turnover ratios, or tax-adjusted returns. You can shoot for the stars without worrying about the cost of taxes on your performance. All gains are taxed equally. But tax-deferred accounts make up only a portion of your portfolio. You can't completely ignore the rules, because you need to know which assets to put in your tax-deferred accounts and which to leave outside.

Let's consider the income you earn on a $2,000 IRA contribution. It may not sound like much—but $2,000 per year adds up over time. $2,000 per year compounding at 10.5% (the long-term historical return for U.S. blue-chip stocks) for 20 years adds up to $133,994. That's more than three times your original investment. Even after paying 28% tax on your gain, you'll net $107,676.

What happens if you invest outside the IRA and pay taxes? If you invest the same $2,000 annually, earn the same 10.5% per year, but pay 28% tax on the earnings, you'll have just $93,774. Income taxes over the 20-year period cost you $13,902 of your gain. (Figures assume we pay taxes out of each year's gains, which are then unavailable for future compounding.)

If you invest the same $2,000 per year at the same 10.5% for 40 years, the difference is even more dramatic. In an IRA, your contributions grow to over $1.121 million. But if you pay taxes on the hypothetical mutual fund, above, your contributions grow to just $819,000. The difference, $302,000, is more than *three times* your total investment.

My favorite example of tax-deferred compounding comes from American history. Peter Minuit, the Donald Trump of 17th-century New York, bought all of Manhattan from the Indians for $24 in 1626. This has long been cited as America's first land swindle. But the real swindlers weren't whom you think. If the Indians had invested that $24 in an IRA earning just 5%, they'd have over $252 *billion* dollars today—enough to buy Manhattan *and* all the buildings. But, if they'd paid taxes at 28%, they'd have just $442 *million* today—less than 2% of the tax-deferred total. Taxes would eat up over *98%* of their growth. That difference over time is huge.

As impressive as these examples are, they're all misleading. They assume that the taxable investment is fully taxable, each and every year. But as we've already seen, that just isn't so. Most investments pay at least a portion of their total return in deferred capital gains. What happens when we look at more realistic tax scenarios?

Let's take another look at that $2,000 IRA. We'll assume the same 10.5% return and the same 28% tax rate. But the taxable fund will pay just 2% in income dividends, taxed as ordinary income, and 3% in capital gains dividends, taxed at 20%. The tax on the taxable fund will be 28% of the income dividend plus 20% of the capital gain dividend, for an overall rate of 11.81%. The reinvested dividends increase your basis in the fund, saving tax when you sell 20 years down the road. And when you sell, the rest of your gain gets the benefit of capital gains rates.

At the end of 20 years, the taxable fund is worth $115,110, while the IRA is worth $133,994. However, if you liquidate both funds and pay tax on our gains, the taxable fund is worth $104,144 and the IRA is worth $107,676. The difference here isn't nearly so dramatic.

Now, let's see what happens if you buy an index fund inside the IRA and outside. We'll assume the fund pays just 1.46% in income dividends and a minuscule 0.66% in capital gains dividends. (Figures reflect 1997 returns for the Vanguard Index 500 fund.) Your tax on the taxable fund will be 28% of the income dividend plus 20% of the capital gain dividend, for an overall rate of 5.15%.

At the end of 20 years, the index fund is worth $125,376, while the IRA is worth the usual $133,994. However, if you liquidate both funds and pay tax on your gains, the index fund is worth $109,770. The IRA is still worth just $107,676. The taxable index fund actually outperforms the tax-deferred IRA! Even though the taxable fund doesn't compound as much, the lower tax rate gives you a higher after-tax return.

Remember, tax-deferred accounts have three significant disadvantages relative to taxable accounts. First, plan withdrawals are taxed as ordinary income. There's no chance to take advantage of lower rates on capital gains. (See the ***note*** below discussing employer stock in a qualified plan for an important exception to this rule.) Second, there's no stepped-up basis for assets held until death. Third, there's a 10% penalty tax for most withdrawals before age 59½. As we've just seen, in some cases, capital gains outweigh tax-deferred compounding. This is even more so after the Taxpayer Relief Act of 1997 cut capital gains rates. Most new investors begin building their portfolios with retirement plan contributions. Since all of this money is tax-deferred, there's no need to choose which investments go where. Stuff as much as you can into the account, and build an appropriate portfolio for your specific needs. But at some point, your portfolio will grow large enough to include investments outside your retirement plan and IRA. This may come from an inheritance, a bonus, or just extra savings. Whatever the source, you'll need to consider which investments to hold in taxable accounts (to take advantage of capital gains) and which to hold in tax-deferred accounts (to take advantage of tax-deferred compounding).

This issue is a surprising source of debate among investment advisors. Some recommend holding the investment with the greatest potential long-term return in the tax-deferred account. The reasoning is that greater long-term returns benefit more from tax deferral. But, as we've seen, this isn't necessarily true. Some investments get no advantage from tax-deferred accounts. In fact, some investments actually return *less* after tax at ordinary rates than if you had held them in a taxable account. The general strategy is this: *hold your least tax-efficient investments in your tax-deferred accounts.*

Since long-term capital gains rates are lower than ordinary income rates, it makes more sense to hold growth stocks and stock funds *outside* the IRA, to avoid converting capital gains into ordinary income. You also get to use your losers to offset your winners. Let your capital gains accrue in taxable accounts where you can take advantage of lower capital gains rates. If you hold those investments until your death, your heirs will receive them with a stepped-up basis equal to their value at the time of your death and escape capital gains tax entirely. Use your IRA to shelter bond interest and other current income.

Different stock investing strategies produce different tax results. So, even if your portfolio consists entirely of stocks, you can arrange your portfolio to take maximum advantage of tax deferral. Large company stocks and value stocks tend to pay higher dividends, which are taxed immediately as ordinary income. Small company stocks and growth stocks tend to pay little or no dividends and return more in the form of capital appreciation, taxed only when you sell your shares. So, tax-deferred accounts make more sense for large-cap and value investing. Leave your small-cap and growth investments in a taxable account.

This rule doesn't always hold true, however, if you're in the 28% tax bracket and up. That's because you can buy money market funds and bonds with a 0% tax rate. If municipal money market and bond taxable equivalent yields net you more than taxable cash and bonds, then the stocks, and not the bonds, are the least efficient investment. In these cases, it makes sense to hold your stocks in your tax-deferred accounts.

This principle applies to all types of tax-sheltered investments, including qualified plans, permanent life insurance, and annuities. Variable annuities have grown hugely popular in recent years as a way to buy stocks without paying current tax. But variable annuities can actually *increase* your tax bill by converting capital gains into ordinary income. And variable annuities charge higher fees than comparable mutual funds that can outweigh the benefit of tax deferral. Make the most of tax deferral by choosing the right investments for your tax-deferred accounts.

Some investment strategies work best in tax-deferred accounts regardless of how the underlying investments are taxed:

- If you trade frequently, try to do as much as you can in your tax-deferred accounts. We saw in Chapter Two how frequent turnover whacks your profit with each sale, even with lower capital gain rates.

- If you like the ogs of the Dow^{sm}, kennel them in your tax-deferred accounts. (See ***Chapter 3.1.3***, "The Dogs of the Dow.")

- Active asset allocation—shifting your money among asset classes in reaction to changing market conditions—generates frequent capital gains from rebalancing. You can confine your active asset allocation to your tax-deferred accounts. Or, you can keep core asset class minimums in taxable accounts and adjust the mix of discretionary asset class balances in your tax-deferred accounts.

- If you try to time the market—switching your entire portfolio between cash, stocks, and bonds—do it in your tax-deferred accounts. Market timing makes little sense in a taxable account because you need to beat the market by enough to cover taxes and expenses just to break even. That's one reason why nobody you know got rich from market timing. It's tough enough to beat the market to start with. It's even tougher to do it with the IRS on your back.

Some investments also work best in tax-deferred accounts regardless of your other holdings:

- High yield bond funds always fare best in tax-deferred accounts because of their high taxable yield. If you're willing to trade credit quality in exchange for higher yield, and you're in the 28% bracket or above, consider municipal junk.

- Balanced funds buy both stocks and bonds, usually in about a 60% stock/40% bond ratio. Balanced funds, asset allocation funds, and "lifestyle" funds, generate higher taxable income than pure stock funds. (Asset allocation funds adjust their portfolio mix in reaction to changing market conditions. These changes generate taxable gains that you should protect in tax-deferred accounts. Lifestyle funds are marketed to specific classes of investors—those with similar risk tolerances, such as "conservative," "moderate," or "aggressive," or those with similar retirement dates, such as 2010, 2020, or 2030. These may be useful training bras for new investors. But they implicitly assume that all investors in those classes want or need the same portfolio. A 50-year-old widow with $10,000 and three kids in college needs a far different portfolio than a 50-year-old bachelor with $500,000.)

- Loan participation funds invest in bank loans tied to the prime rate. Since the loan payment resets as the prime rate moves, there's little or no change in principal value, and nearly all of these funds' returns come in the form of current income.
- Market neutral funds and bear funds are special categories of stock funds designed to eliminate or profit from the risk of market declines. (See *Chapter 4.5*, "Managed Money Alternatives.")

Let's put it all together. Which investments should you direct to which accounts?

- First, contribute as much as it takes to claim the maximum match from your employer retirement plan. That's free money you'd be foolish to pass up. If your investment choices are lousy, find the one that stinks the least and petition your employer for better choices.
- Next, examine your IRA alternatives to see which choice is best—an ordinary deductible IRA or Roth IRA. If a Roth makes more sense, contribute as much as you can. If an ordinary IRA makes more sense, then continue funding your tax-deferred accounts. If you like the choices in your employer retirement account, fine, keep filling it. If you'd prefer your own investment choices, contribute to your own IRA.
- Finally, look at which investments are most efficient for you and your particular tax bracket. If you're in the 15% bracket, hold inefficient investments (cash and taxable bonds) in tax-deferred accounts and more efficient stocks in taxable accounts. If you're in the 28% bracket or above, hold stocks in tax-deferred accounts and municipal bonds in

taxable accounts. If you're buying inefficient investments, contribute as much as you can to IRAs, employer retirement plans, and variable annuities, in that order, to create a tax-deferred pool for those investments. If you're buying more efficient investments, do it in taxable accounts to take advantage of lower capital gains rates. You might also want to keep a taxable account that you can tap with a margin loan in case of an emergency.

Many retirement plans and variable annuities offer a fixed account or stable value fund that works like a bank CD. Fixed accounts promise to pay a fixed rate for a fixed period of time and guarantee your principal against loss. Stable value funds buy intermediate term debt and guaranteed investment contracts to pay higher interest than money markets with no principal fluctuation. These accounts combine the return of an intermediate-term bond fund with the principal stability of cash. Many observers criticize retirement plan investors for putting too much of their assets into fixed accounts and not enough into stocks. But fixed accounts and stable value funds remain excellent, if overlooked, places for the cash portion of your portfolio. These accounts actually let you invest more of your portfolio in volatile assets such as stocks because the stable asset value protects so well against market downturns.

Choosing to contribute to tax-deferred accounts can also depend on a more personal issue; specifically, your tax bracket today relative to your tax bracket tomorrow. It may make sense to ignore the above rules if the two will be significantly different. Consider the choice of whether to contribute to a deductible IRA. If you're in the 28% bracket today, and you know you'll be in the 15% bracket when you withdraw your money from your account, it makes sense to save 28% today and pay 15% tomorrow, even with a tax-efficient investment. Similarly, if you're in the 15% bracket today, and you know you'll be in the 28% bracket tomorrow, it makes no sense to save 15% today if you'll owe nearly twice that much down the road. The Taxpayer Relief Act of 1997 changed the rules here by extending the benefit of capital gains treatment to taxpayers in the 15% and 28% bracket. So you need to consider whether the deduction you get today is worth the extra taxes you'll pay tomorrow.

Unfortunately, figuring your tax bracket tomorrow isn't as easy as it sounds. For starters, you probably won't know exactly what your income is going to be. You don't know how your investments will perform between now and retirement, so you don't know how much you can count on them to produce. Next, you can find yourself in a *higher* bracket even if your income drops. You'll probably lose most of your deductions, which in turn will boost your taxable income. If your house is paid off and your kids have graduated from college, you can find yourself paying more tax just because you lose those deductions. You'll also have to start withdrawing money from your retirement accounts by April 1 of the year after the year in which you reach age 70½. This will increase your income and possibly your tax bracket as well. Finally, even if you could predict your future taxable income, there's no way to guarantee that Congress won't change the rates between now and then.

Investing for retirement—stuffing today's income into risky investments and trusting the markets to provide tomorrow's living—is hard. Pulling money *out* is the fun part. But even then it's important to choose which accounts to tap when you take your money out. If most of your investments are in tax-deferred accounts, your choice will be easy. Take the income you need and pay the tax. But if some accounts are taxable and others are tax-deferred, you'll have to choose which accounts to tap and drain first:

- If you want to preserve your savings as long as possible, draw down taxable accounts first. The extra tax you pay on withdrawals from tax-deferred accounts makes it more expensive to net the same spendable income than from taxable accounts.
- If you want to maximize the amount you leave to your heirs, consider tapping tax-deferred accounts first. At your death, your heirs will

receive assets from your taxable accounts with a stepped-up basis equal to their value at your date of death. This is even more valuable if your taxable account includes stocks that you don't plan to sell. The stocks will continue to grow tax-deferred, and the only disad-vantage relative to tax-deferred accounts is the tax on the dividends. If you really do hold them 'til death do you part, your heirs will enjoy the stepped-up basis your tax-deferred accounts can't give.

- If your retirement income is high enough to subject your Social Security benefits to tax, consider consuming principal from your tax-able accounts to generate cash while preserving your Social Security benefits. (See *Chapter 6.5*, "Social Security.") I know that your mother told you never to dip into principal. But if she's so smart, how come she isn't rich?

- If your 97-year-old grandmother is still around to scare you with stories from the Great Depression, consider investing a part of your nest egg in an immediate annuity for an income you can't outlive. As life expectancies climb, preserving income will become more and more important. And it won't matter how efficiently you can invest if you run out of money. This is especially true if you're blessed (or cursed) with Methuselah's genes.

Is your IRA large enough to generate all the income you need? Here's a slick strategy for assuring you never run out of money *and* holding income and estate taxes to a minimum: simply annuitize your IRA. (For more information on annuitizing, see *Chapter 7.2.1*, "Immediate Annuities." This offers three powerful advantages:

- You can invest the rest of your portfolio—your taxable assets—in stocks You won't need to generate income from stocks or bonds. And you won't need to worry that a stock market slide could cost you income during your lifetime.

- If you need more income, you can sell some of your stock. This will pay you with tax-free principal and long-term capital gains. Or you can margin your stocks for tax-free loan proceeds and create an estate tax deduction at the same time.

- You'll keep down the tax on your outside portfolio since you won't have to pay unless you choose to sell. When you do, you'll have the chance to profit from lower long-term gain rates.

- You'll leave more to your heirs. They won't have to pay income tax on your IRA, and there won't be estate tax. Your outside portfolio will likely be worth more invested in stocks than if it included, stocks, bonds, and cash. And your heirs will be happier with a fat stock portfolio and a stepped-up basis than they would with the massive tax liability of an inherited IRA.

- Annuitizing your IRA, so that the income stops at your death, removes the value of the IRA from your estate. You can't profit from the "stretchout" IRA we'll discuss later. But this may be less a blow to your heirs than you think. At your death, your heirs owe federal, state, and local income taxes, plus federal and state estate taxes, on the entire account balance. This typically eats up 80-90% of its value. One writer has even calculated that New York City residents can die owing over 100% of their IRA balance in tax.

This strategy certainly isn't for everyone. But if you're comfortable with the stock market and you're willing to let your winners ride, you can save a bundle for yourself and your heirs.

6.2 Qualified Retirement Plans

A qualified retirement plan is one that your employer maintains that qualifies for special tax treatment. Qualified retirement plans are divided into two categories: defined benefit plans, which promise a predetermined annual benefit, usually based on your salary and length of service, and defined contribution plans, such as today's popular 401(k)s, whose ultimate benefit will depend on how much you and your employer contribute to the plan and how your investments perform. Employers are shifting away from traditional defined benefit plans and shifting the responsibility for accumulating retirement savings onto employees. Clearly this is cheaper for the employer. But for our purposes, the real distinction is between trustee-directed plans, where the trustee manages your account, and participant-directed accounts, where you manage your own money. Employers aren't just shifting the burden of saving money—they're also shifting the burden of *managing* it. This is also cheaper for your employer—it takes the trustee off the hook for your investment choices (They're still liable for selecting investment options they offered in the plan.)

Trustee-directed plans include defined benefit plans, profit sharing plans, and money purchase plans where the trustee makes the investment decisions. In these cases, you'll have no opportunity to manage your account. This makes it difficult to integrate your retirement account holdings into your overall portfolio. You won't have up-to-date information on specific securities. And you're limited to broad categories in your overall asset allocation.

Participant-directed plans require you to manage your own account. The transition from old-style defined benefit plans to today's 401(k) plans is turning us into a nation of pension fund managers. These plans ask us to determine how much we need to save, integrate our pension investments into our overall asset allocation, monitor shifting economic and financial news, and use this information to guarantee our own retirement security. It will be interesting to see if we succeed. Don't make the mistake of managing your retirement account as a separate portfolio.

If your employer wants to avoid fiduciary liability for your investment performance, the trustee will have to provide you with two specific opportunities. First, you'll need the opportunity to exercise meaningful control over your account. This means you'll need timely information about investment options, fees, managers, and the like. Second, you'll need at least three different investment choices with materially different risk and reward characteristics. Three is just the minimum; most plans provide more. Some plans provide over 100 fund choices, and some sophisticated self-directed 401(k) plans actually give you a brokerage account to buy individual securities.

If your plan offers employer stock, you can take advantage of lower long-term capital gains rates when you sell the stock. However, even if your company's stock has a long track record of steady growth, avoid overloading your account. Remember, it's important to diversify, to avoid putting all your eggs in one basket. This is especially true with your employer. If business sours and you lose your job, you can find your retirement account balance vanishing along with your income—exactly when you need it most.

In most cases, you should contribute as much as you can to your plan. That's because your employer will usually match a portion of your contribution. Contribute as much as it takes to maximize that match! The combination of immediate tax savings, employer matches, and tax deferral is the closest most of us will get to a Powerball win. In some cases, though, it doesn't pay to max out your contribution. This is true in cases where the new Roth IRA makes sense. If your tax bracket now is low, it may make sense to forego today's deductible contribution in favor of tomorrow's tax-free income. And many investors should contribute as much as they can to maximize their match, then fund a Roth IRA, before contributing any more to their employer plan.

Let's say you make $50,000 per year, and you're in the 28% tax bracket. Your employer offers a 401(k) and matches contributions 50% up to 4% of salary. You'd like to save $2,000 per year towards retirement in a stock account earning 10.5% per year. Should you contribute to the 401(k), open an IRA, buy taxable mutual funds, or buy a variable annuity? You don't need to crunch the numbers to see that the 401(k) is the clear winner. It's the only choice that offers an immediate tax break, an employer match, and tax-deferred growth.

You might be reluctant to contribute as much as you can. What if you lock up money you might need for a down payment on a house, or for medical emergencies? Fortunately, most plans give you escape hatches in the form of loans, hardship withdrawals, and in-service withdrawals.

- Plan loans let you tap your money without giving up tax-deferral. They also give you access to your money it before age 59½ without the usual 10% early withdrawal penalty. You can borrow up to $50,000 or 50% of your vested account balance, whichever is less. (If your plan is particularly flexible, you can borrow up to 100% of your plan balance by putting up extra security, such as your house.) You have to repay your loan within five years (20 years if you use it to buy a primary residence), with substantially level installments paid at least quarterly. If you leave your job before you repay the loan, you'll owe tax on the unpaid balance unless you repay the loan with funds from another source. Plan loan interest isn't tax deductible—you'll repay the loan with after-tax dollars, then pay tax again when you withdraw your repayment dollars from the plan.

- Some 401(k) and 403(b) plans also let you take a hardship withdrawal of your own contributions (but not employer contributions or earnings) for an immediate and heavy financial need—usually defined to include unreimbursed medical bills, a down payment on a house, college costs, and payment of any amount needed to prevent eviction or foreclosure on your primary residence. If your plan allows both loans and hardship withdrawals, you have to borrow the maximum amount available before taking a hardship withdrawal. And, if you do take a hardship withdrawal, you can't contribute to the plan for the next year.

- Finally, some profit sharing and 401(k) plans let you make in-service withdrawals while you still work for the company. You can take the withdrawal in cash (after you pay tax and a 10% penalty, if applicable), or you can roll the withdrawal into an IRA. Rolling your qualified plan balance into an IRA may be the solution if you don't like your plan's investment options.

By some estimates, at least one-third of 401(k) participants have loans against their accounts, with an average loan balance of $6,000. It's best to think of loans and hardship withdrawals as emergency escape hatches. They aren't there to help you buy a car or a bass boat. But they should give you some comfort that you can take money out in case of emergency. This should give you the confidence to make the most of your employer retirement plan. For more information, see your plan administrator.

Employer Stock in Your Qualified Plan

Employer stock you hold in a qualified plan gets special tax treatment that lets you take advantage of lower capital gains rates when you sell. Rolling your employer stock into an IRA can be the biggest mistake you'll ever make—and cost you thousands I tax you don't need to pay.

You have two choices when it comes time to take your employer stock from your employer's plan:

- If you roll your employer stock into an IRA, you'll pay no tax now. You'll pay no current tax on your dividend income. And you'll pay tax at ordinary rates withdrawals.
- If you take your employer stock outright, you'll pay tax at ordinary rates now on the stock's value at the time it was contributed to the plan. You'll also pay tax at ordinary rates on your dividend income. But when you sell the stock, you'll pay tax at lower long-term capital gains rates on the appreciation since the date of contribution. (If your stock is worth less now than when it was contributed to the plan, you'll owe tax at ordinary income rates on the full value when you take the distribution.) *And*, any unrealized appreciation above $50,000 qualifies for a stepped-up basis at death.

It may make sense to pay tax now on the value of the stock at the time it was contributed to the plan in exchange for lower capital gains rates on the appreciation when you finally sell. Let's say your plan balance includes 100 shares of stock worth $10 per share when contributed. The stock is now worth $30 per share, and you're in the 28% bracket. If you roll the stock into an IRA, you'll pay no tax now. But you'll pay $8.40 per share if you sell and withdraw your money (28% of $30). In contrast, if you take the stock outright, you'll owe $2.80 per share (28% of the $10 value at the time it was contributed to the plan). But if you sell, you'll owe just $4.00 tax on the $20 appreciation, for a total tax bill of $6.80. This is nearly 20% less tax than if you roll the stock into the IRA.

This rule suggests several strategies:

- If you plan to sell stock now to diversify, consider rolling the portion you plan to sell into an IRA. You'll get to sell and diversify without paying immediate tax. This can be even more valuable if you plan to use the proceeds to buy less efficient investments such as bonds.
- If you plan to sell stock to raise cash, take the stock outright. You'll benefit from lower capital gains rates on the portion of stock you sell.

You can also take stock outright and use it to secure a loan to raise cash without selling at all.

- If you've acquired stock at different values over the course of your employment, you can pick and choose which shares to take now and which to roll into the IRA. That way, you can take advantage of capital gains rates on older shares with a lower cost basis, while rolling the rest into your IRA.

- This rule also affects your investment choices if you manage your retirement account while you're still employed. If you sell employer stock and transfer the assets into a different investment option, you'll destroy your ability to profit from lower capital gains rates after retirement.

This issue presents a huge conflict of interest if you're rolling your employer plan into an IRA with a full-service stockbroker, financial planner, or money manager. If you take your stock directly, your advisor can't make commissions or generate asset-management fees from it. Unscrupulous advisors might recommend that you roll your employer stock into *their* program—in order to boost *their* fees—at the expense of your tax break. (Ignorant advisors might not even know about the rule!) Be *very* careful before you commit to rolling your employer stock into an IRA—and get an unbiased second opinion.

6.3 Self-Employed Plans

If you're self-employed, either as a sole proprietor, partner, or owner of a corporation, you have several retirement-plan choices you can use to create tax-deferred investment accounts. If you have no employees, choose the plan that lets you make the largest contribution you can. If you have employees, your choice depends on how much you want to contribute for them.

The same rules apply with self-employed retirement plans as with any other tax-deferred account. Contribute when the combination of up-front tax breaks and tax deferral makes sense. And use them for your least tax-efficient investments. Here are the various plans:

- A Savings Incentive Match Plan for Employees, or SIMPLE plan, is an expanded IRA that allows you and your employees to contribute more than the usual $2,000 limit. In this case, you can contribute 100% of net income up to $6,000. You have to match each employee's contribution dollar-for-dollar up to 3% of compensation, or make a 2% nondiscretionary contribution for each employee.
- A Simplified Employee Pension, or SEP, is another expanded IRA that lets you contribute more than $2,000. In this case, the limit is 15% of your income from the business, up to the "covered compensation limit" ($170,000 for 2000). (If you're a sole proprietor or partner, the limit is 13.04% of your net self-employment income, minus half of your self-employment tax, up to the covered compensation limit). You'll have to contribute something for your employees. However, you can choose an integrated plan that allows you to increase your contribution to yourself and other highly compensated employees by up to 5.7% of income above a certain floor.
- A profit-sharing Keogh lets you make discretionary contributions of up to 15% of net income (13.04% for sole proprietors or partners). You can vary the contribution each years; there's no requirement to commit a fixed sum or percentage. You'll have to contribute something for all eligible employees; however, you can choose an integrated or cross-tested plan to contribute more on your own behalf (see below).
- A money purchase Keogh lets you make fixed contributions of up to 25% of net income (20% of gross income for sole proprietors and

partners). This is appropriate if you can commit a fixed sum each year. Many businesses adopt paired profit sharing and money purchase Keoghs for flexibility to contribute between 10% and 25% per year.

- Integrated and cross-tested plans let you contribute more on behalf of yourself and your highly compensated employees—generally, those who own more than 5% of the business or who make more than $85,000 per year (plan years ending in 2000). One type of cross-tested plan, the "age-weighted" plan, is most valuable for owners more than 15 years older than the average employee.

- A defined benefit Keogh lets you contribute whatever amount necessary to fund a defined income of up to $130,000 per year beginning at a defined retirement age. These plans are more difficult and expensive to administer. But once you reach age 45 or thereabouts, a defined benefit plan can give you a far bigger tax break than the defined contribution alternatives.

You can also set up a nonqualified deferred compensation plan. This is simply a promise by the business to pay a benefit at a later date. There's no requirement that you actually fund the promise. But many plans buy life insurance on the executive who will receive the benefit. This avoids tax on the annual gains, and the business can use insurance proceeds to recover the cost of the deferred compensation itself at the executive's death.

6.4 IRAs

Congress established IRAs in 1974 to encourage retirement savings. Since then, account balances have soared past the trillion-dollar mark. Congress sharply limited the deduction for IRA contributions in 1986. But millions of Americans still contribute faithfully each year. What's more, tax law changes have spawned a whole zoo of IRAs. There are now regular deductible IRAs, nondeductible IRAs, spousal IRAs, Roth IRAs, rollover IRAs, conduit IRAs, and even education IRAs. IRAs gives you the same tax-deferred growth as an employer retirement plan. But you get more flexibility to manage your account because you aren't limited to your employer's investment choices.

Managing your IRA is a complicated subject, and you can read entire books on taking cash from your account. Congress complicated matters with The Taxpayer Relief Act of 1997 and the introduction of new Roth IRAs. This discussion will help you determine how much tax you can save by contributing, and how much tax you'll owe on required minimum distributions. This Chapter lays out the basic rules for the most common choices, ordinary IRAs and Roth IRAs.

6.4.1 Ordinary IRAs

Ordinary IRAs let you deduct up to $2,000 from today's income (subject to certain qualifications) and compound your earnings tax-deferred for retirement:

- Anyone with earned income from salary, self-employment, or the like, can contribute to an IRA.
- You can contribute 100% of your earned income up to $2,000.
- If you don't actively participate in an employer retirement plan, you can deduct your contribution as an adjustment to income regardless of how much you make. If you do participate in an employer retirement plan, you can deduct your contribution if your AGI falls within certain limits. For 2000, you can deduct all of your contribution if your AGI is below $32,000 (single filers) or $52,000 (joint filers, and part of your contribution if your AGI falls below $42,000 (single filers) or

$62,000 (joint filers). These limits increase by $1,000 each year through 2003, then increase in larger jumps through 2007.

IRA Deduction Limits		
Year	Phase-out Range (Single Filers)	Phase-out Range (Joint Filers)
1999	$31,000 - $41,000	$51,000 - $61,000
2000	$32,000 - $42,000	$52,000 - $62,000
2001	$33,000 - $43,000	$53,000 - $64,000
2002	$34,000 - $44,000	$54,000 - $64,000
2003	$40,000 - $50,000	$60,000 - $70,000
2004	$45,000 - $55,000	$65,000 - $75,000
2005	$50,000 - $60,000	$70,000 - $80,000
2006	$50,000 - $60,000	$75,000 - $85,000
2007	$50,000 - $60,000	$80,000 - $100,000

- You have to contribute cash. You can't transfer securities from another account.
- You can put almost any investment in an IRA: bank deposits, stocks, bonds, mutual funds, real estate, mortgages and other loans, private placements, even limited partnerships. About the only things you can't buy are most collectibles (rugs, wine, stamps, etc.), and certain options and futures investments.
- It pays to contribute early. You can put your money in as early as January 1 or as late as April 15 of the next year. If you contribute on January 1 and earn a steady 10.5% return, your contribution will already be worth $2,276 by the next year's April 15 deadline.
- If you take out money before age 59½ you'll owe ordinary income tax plus a 10% penalty tax on withdrawals. (See *Chapter 6.4.7*, "Early Withdrawals," for exceptions to this rule.)
- Once you reach age 59½ you can withdraw money as ordinary income. (Your custodian will report your withdrawals on Form 1099-R.) The entire withdrawal is taxed as ordinary income, unless you've made nondeductible contributions (see below).

- You have to start taking money out by April 1 of the year after you reach age 70½.
- When you die, your IRA passes to your designated beneficiary and avoids probate.
- You can deduct your IRA account fee as a miscellaneous itemized deduction if you pay it separately by check, rather than from plan assets.

Don't overlook the power of that $2,000 annual deduction. If you're in the 28% tax bracket, your $2,000 annual contribution saves you $560 in federal income tax. In effect, your $2,000 contribution costs just $1,440. If your account grows for 20 years at 8%, the IRA will grow to $58,846 than it would in a fully taxable account. If you invest your $560 tax savings in a taxable side fund, the additional investment will grow to $21,233. That's more than $80,000 difference out of a mere $2,000 deduction.

IRA sponsors report contributions to the IRS, so if you don't make your contribution by the April 15 deadline, don't just take the deduction and hope for the best. IRS computers can crosscheck your return against contributions to verify the deduction.

6.4.2 Nondeductible IRAs

If you actively participate in an employer retirement plan and your income exceeds these limits, you can still contribute to a nondeductible IRA and get tax-deferred compounding without the up-front deduction. Use *Form 8606* to report these contributions. Keep a copy of each *Form 8606* you file over the years. When you start taking money out, each withdrawal will include a nontaxable portion of your total nondeductible contribution. To determine this tax-free portion, divide the amount of nondeductible contributions by the total of all your IRA account balances. Each year, as you withdraw money, your nondeductible balance will shrink by the tax-free portions of each year's withdrawals. To determine future tax-free portions, divide the total of unrecovered nondeductible contributions by the total account balance.

Let's say that in 1990, 1991, and 1992, you make a total of $6,000 in nondeductible contributions. Now the account is worth $20,000 and you'd like to take out $2,000. Since $6,000 of the $20,000 balance, or 30%, is from nondeductible contributions, 30% of your $2,000 withdrawal, or $600, is tax-free.

Next year, your account grows back to $20,000. You'd like to take out another $2,000. Since just $5,400 of your $20,000 balance, or 27%, remains from nondeductible contributions, 27% of your $2,000 withdrawal, or $540, is tax-free.

Many financial advisors discourage nondeductible contributions to avoid these accounting hassles. It would be easier if you could simply withdraw nondeductible contributions in a single lump sum—but you can't. And it would be easier if the IRS or your custodian did the paperwork—but they don't. Still, a nondeductible IRA may make sense *if* you can't make a deductible contribution, *if* you don't qualify for a Roth IRA, *if* you still want to make tax-deferred investments without the extra costs of life insurance and annuities, and *if* you don't mind the extra paperwork.

6.4.3 Spousal IRAs

Nonworking spouses can put up to $2,000 into a spousal IRA. The couple's combined income, minus the working spouse's own IRA contribution, has to be enough to cover the nonworking spouse contribution. If the working spouse doesn't actively participate in an employer retirement plan, the nonworking spouse can contribute $2,000 regardless of the couple's income. If the working spouse does participate in an employer retirement plan, the nonworking spouse can contribute so long as the couple's AGI is $150,000 or less. Otherwise, the rules are the same as with ordinary IRAs.

6.4.4 Roth IRAs

Roth IRAs are a new form of IRA with a "back-end" tax advantage: contributions aren't deductible; but withdrawals are tax free if earnings are held in the account for at least five years and you have reached age 59½. Here's how they work:

- You can contribute to a Roth IRA, regardless of whether you participate in an employer plan, if your AGI is less than $110,000 ($160,000 for joint filers). Contributions are phased out between $95,000 and $110,000 ($150,000 and $160,000 for joint filers).
- You can contribute up to $2,000 per year to a Roth IRA.
- Roth IRA contributions aren't deductible.
- You have to contribute cash; you can't transfer securities from another account.
- You can put almost any investment in a Roth IRA: bank deposits, stocks, bonds, mutual funds, real estate, mortgages and other loans, private placements, even limited partnerships. About the only things you can't buy are most collectibles (rugs, wine, stamps, etc.), and certain options and futures investments.
- It pays to contribute early. You can contribute as early as January 1 or as late as April 15 of the following year. If you contribute on January 1 and earn a steady 10.5% return, your contribution will already be worth $2,276 by the April 15 deadline.

- You can withdraw funds without taxes or penalties once you've reached age 59½ and held the funds in the Roth IRA for five *tax* years after the year in which you make your initial contribution. For example, on April 15, 1999, you open a Roth IRA for the 1998 tax year. The five-year period expires January 1, 2003, even though five calendar years haven't passed.
- Premature withdrawals are treated first as original deposits, then earnings. That means you can with-draw your original deposits without paying any tax. Once you start withdrawing earnings, you'll owe ordinary income tax plus the usual 10% penalty if you're under age 59½. For example, you contribute $2,000 per year for three years and your account grows to $7,000. You can withdraw $6,000 (your original contribution) tax and penalty-free. If you withdraw the $1,000 growth, you'll owe ordinary tax on that amount (because the account is less than five years old), plus the 10% penalty if you're under 59½.
- There are no required distributions from a Roth IRA as there are for a regular deductible IRA, nondeductible IRA, or spousal IRA.
- You can continue contributing to a Roth IRA even after reaching age 70½.
- At death, your Roth IRA passes to your designated beneficiaries without passing through probate. Your beneficiaries can withdraw the entire balance, tax-free. Or they can leave the balance in the account up to five years or withdraw the money, tax-free, over their own life expectancies.
- Withdrawals from Roth IRAs are tax-free in states that structure their tax code after the federal code, as well as those with no state income tax.

6.4.5 Choose the Right IRA

Which IRA is best for you, the ordinary IRA with the up-front deduction or the Roth IRA with the tax-free income? This depends on two questions. First, what is your tax rate now, compared to where it will be when you need the money? And second, what will you do with the taxes you save if you take your deduction up front? The choice is easy if you don't qualify for a tax-deductible ordinary IRA. In that case, choose the Roth IRA if you can. However, if you don't actively participate in an employer retirement plan, or if your income allows you to choose between an ordinary IRA and a Roth IRA, you have a dilemma.

If your tax rate is the same going in and out, you'll net the same amount whether you pay now, as with a Roth IRA, or later, as with an ordinary IRA. Let's say you're in the 28% tax bracket and you have $2,000 to invest. You can invest the full $2,000, then pay tax on your withdrawal. Or, you can pay $560 in tax, invest the remaining $1,440, then pay no tax on your withdrawal. Either way you'll net the same amount down the road. You pay the same 28% on your principal today, with the Roth IRA, as you would tomorrow with the ordinary IRA.

The picture changes depending on what you do with your IRA tax savings. If you can afford to invest your savings, you'll have more money down the road by choosing the deductible IRA and stuffing your savings into a side fund. Let's say you have $2,000 of income to invest. You can invest the full $2,000 in an ordinary IRA, or $1,440 in a Roth IRA. But if you choose the deductible IRA, you'll have $560 in tax savings. If you can invest the tax savings in a side fund, you'll have more down the road with that choice. The after-tax withdrawal from the ordinary IRA gives you the same meat-and-potatoes as the tax-free withdrawal from the Roth IRA. The side fund gives you extra gravy, even invested in a taxable account.

Now let's say that you can afford to invest the full $2,000 in either account. This is an easy case. Your $2,000 investment grows to the same amount in either IRA. At the end, you'll owe tax on your ordinary IRA balance. But there won't be any tax on your Roth IRA balance. Clearly, the Roth IRA wins. It wins even if you invest your $560 tax savings in a side fund. That's because you'll owe tax on your side fund. You could even the race some by investing your side fund in a tax-deferred vehicle such as a variable annuity. Still, the Roth IRA will almost always leave you with more.

The Roth IRA nets you more because it actually lets you invest more of your income. This is true even though the limit for both contributions is $2,000. Here's why. Let's say you're in the 28% tax bracket. If you contribute to an ordinary IRA, it costs you $2,000 dollars before tax to invest $2,560 (your $2,000 contribution plus your $560 tax break). If you contribute to a Roth IRA, it costs you $2,777.77 before tax to invest $2,000 (your $2,000 investment plus $777.77 in tax). We saw earlier that your after-tax net is the same whether you pay your tax up front or when you take your money out. But in this case you have *different* investments. With the ordinary IRA, your pre-tax pot is $2,560. With the Roth IRA, your pre-tax pot is $2,777.77. Since taxes take the same percentage of both pots, the $2,777.77 pot naturally nets you more. This effect increases as your investments have more time to grow. The same principal applies in the case of Roth IRA conversions.

The picture changes if your tax rates are different going in and going out. If your future tax rate will be lower, you'll be better off taking the high deduction now and paying the lower tax later. Take the deduction now when it's worth more. It makes no sense to pass up 28% now to save 15% down the road. Similarly, if your future tax rate will be higher, you'll wind up better foregoing a low deduction now and saving the higher tax later. Save the tax break for then. It makes no sense to save 15% now, then pay 28% down the road.

What's more, your money going in may get you a deduction now at your highest rate. But your money coming out will likely be taxed at your average rate. That's because your future withdrawals will make up a larger portion of your total income than your contributions today. Your $2,000 contribution today probably saves tax at your highest rate. It's not large enough to lower your tax bracket. But when you take money out down the road, you'll get the advantage of deductions, exemptions, and moving up through the brackets *before* you finally pay tax at your highest rate. So don't just look at your likely marginal rate for taking money out. Look at your likely *average* rate for a more realistic comparison.

Plenty of financial services companies have created IRA calculators purporting to show you, down to the dollar, which choice is best for you. These are available for computers, as well as plain old pencils and paper. The problem, of course, is that you don't know what your future tax rate will be! Even if you're retired now, your tax rate will probably change before you've cleaned everything out. These calculators are useful only when they show dramatically different results. If you do choose to crunch the numbers, run several comparisons using different future tax rates to see how changing assumptions affect your results.

Bottom line: if you think tomorrow's tax rate will be lower than today's, choose a deductible IRA for higher immediate tax savings. If you think tomorrow's rate will be the same as today's, choose the Roth IRA if you can afford to invest the full $2,000. Finally, if you think tomorrow's rate will rise, choose the Roth IRA for tax-free income.

6.4.6 Roth IRA Conversions

You can convert your existing IRA into a Roth IRA if your adjusted gross income in the year you convert is less than $100,000. If you convert, you'll have to report the value of your account on the date of conversion (minus any nondeductible contributions) as taxable income the year you convert. Should you take the offer?

The answer here turns on the same issues as the choice between IRAs for new money. First, where will your tax bracket be when you take out the money, compared to where it is now? And second, where will you find the money to pay the tax?

First, let's see what happens if your tax rate stays the same. Let's assume your tax rate now is 28%. Down the road your withdrawals from an ordinary IRA will also be taxed at 28%. If you use part of your IRA balance to pay the tax you'll owe on conversion, there's no difference whether you pay tax now to convert, or wait until retirement. Remember, as long as the tax you pay now is the same as the tax you avoid in the future, it doesn't matter when you actually pay. Your after-tax total remains the same.

But if you can pay the tax from somewhere else, you'll have more money down the road by converting to a Roth IRA and paying your taxes from the outside source. Paying the tax from the outside source is like investing your tax savings in a side fund. It has the same effect as if you had contributed an amount equal to the tax in a lump sum to your ordinary IRA now. Let's say you have $100,000 to convert. Your tax on the conversion will be $28,000. Paying the tax from an outside source will give you the same result down the road as if you had dumped that $28,000 into the IRA itself, then paid 28% tax on withdrawals down the road.

The picture changes again if your tax rates are different today and tomorrow. If today's tax is *higher* than tomorrow's, don't convert. Why pay today's high tax rate to save tomorrow's low tax? But if today's tax is *lower*, convert. Why not pay 15% today to save 28% later?

Unfortunately, you can't just look at marginal rates today versus tomorrow:

- First, the amount you convert will probably be taxed at a *higher* rate than today's marginal rate. That's because you add the amount you convert to your regular taxable income. This extra income may be enough to push you into an even higher tax bracket. Why convert an enormous account, and add it to this year's income, if it means paying 39.6% today to save 28% or 31% down the road? The extra income might also be enough to phase out deductions and credits, or subject your Social Security benefits to tax. You might want to convert just part of your account each year, or wait for a year when you have less income elsewhere.

- Second, the future income you take from an ordinary IRA will probably be taxed at a *lower* rate than tomorrow's marginal rate. Remember, your IRA will grow over time. Your future withdrawals will make up a larger portion of your total income than your contributions today. Today's contribution probably saves tax at your highest rate. It's not enough to lower your tax bracket. But, your future withdrawals won't all be taxed at your highest rate. If they make up a substantial portion of your total income, some will be taxed at less than your highest rate. So, you need to know what your *average* rate will be when you take out your money.

Remember to consider these adjustments when you think about converting. Even if today's rate and tomorrow's rate appear the same, they probably aren't. This means that conversion isn't the slam-dunk so many taxpayers thought it would be when the Roth IRA first appeared. And most Roth IRA conversion calculators—especially the cheap cardboard slide rules—are hopelessly ill equipped to consider these important adjustments.

If you have employer stock in a qualified plan that you'd like to roll into a Roth IRA, think hard before you convert. If you roll the stock into an IRA, you'll owe tax at ordinary rates on the entire value of the stock when you convert. Dividends and future appreciation will be tax-free. But if you take the stock outright, you'll owe tax at ordinary rates on the stock's value at the time it was contributed to the plan, plus tax at capital gains rates on the appreciation when you sell. Why pay ordinary rates now when you can pay less *and* pay later?

Finally, if you choose to convert to a Roth IRA, you may owe under-payment penalties if your withholding and quarterly estimates aren't enough to cover your total tax bill, including the amount due on the conversion. Your combined withholding and quarterly estimates should equal 100% of your tax due for the year. There will be no penalty if the amount underwithheld is $1,000 or less, and no penalty if the amount withheld is at least 100% of your previous year's tax liability. If regular withholding and quarterly estimates don't appear to cover the bill, you can begin making quarterly estimates for the quarter in which you convert the account.

Consider converting your ordinary IRA to a Roth IRA if: 1) the tax you would pay to convert today is less than the tax you would pay on an ordinary IRA withdrawal tomorrow; 2) the income you report by converting doesn't boost your current tax rate; and 3) you can pay the tax with funds from outside the IRA itself. Also consider converting if you're more concerned with maximizing the income available to your heirs than you are with today's income. Since Roth IRAs don't require minimum distributions, you can leave more money to accumulate in a Roth IRA.

You can also convert the *part* of your account that meets the above guidelines each year for as long as it takes to finish the job. Let's say you have a $100,000 account you want to convert. But converting, and paying tax, on more than $20,000 of it would push you into a higher tax bracket and erase the advantage of converting the amount above $20,000. Or, you can convert $30,000, but your outside assets aren't enough to pay tax on more than $20,000. Convert as much as you can within your present tax bracket and available funds and repeat the process until you're done.

If you believe Congress will adopt a flat tax system with no tax on investment income, don't convert. Why pay tax now if Congress will let you take it all tax-free tomorrow? (If you really think Congress will give up the power to buy votes with tax legislation, you probably still believe in the Tooth Fairy.)

6.4.7 Early Withdrawals

IRAs are intended as long-term retirement accounts, not merely tax-deferred savings accounts. So, the IRS imposes a 10% penalty on most withdrawals before age 59½. Fortunately, there are several ways to access funds from your IRA without paying the 10% penalty:

- There's no penalty to withdraw money on account of death or total and permanent disability. Of course, death won't help you, and disability is a steep price to avoid a 10% tax.
- There's no penalty to withdraw money from a regular IRA (but not a Roth IRA) to pay for unreimbursed medical expenses (up to the amount allowed as a medical expense deduction). This sounds attractive, but it's really quite impractical. The deduction is limited to medical expenses over 7.5% of AGI. But how do you know what your medical costs will be? And how do you know what AGI will be? Don't forget, the amount you withdraw from the IRA increases your AGI, cutting that medical expense deduction even further.
- There's no penalty for withdrawals of up to $10,000 (lifetime maximum) used within 120 days of the withdrawal for qualified acquisition costs of a first-time homebuyer's principal residence. You're a first-time homebuyer if neither you nor your spouse have owned a primary residence in the last two years.
- There's no penalty to withdraw money for higher education expenses, including tuition, room and board, fees, books, supplies, supplies, and required equipment. You can use this loophole to withdraw money for yourself, your spouse, and your dependants.
- There's no penalty to withdraw money if you're retired and over age 55.
- There's no penalty or tax to transfer money to a divorcing spouse under a qualified domestic relation order.

If you need money for a short time, simply take it from your IRA and redeposit it in a *different* IRA within 60 days. The redeposit qualifies as a rollover and there will be no tax or penalty due at all. You can use this strategy once within a 12-month period.

If you need to withdraw funds from a regular IRA (but not a Roth IRA), you can avoid the 10% penalty if you annuitize your account, or take the funds in a series of substantially equal payments over your life expectancy. You'll still owe ordinary tax on the withdrawals, but you'll avoid the 10% penalty. The catch is that you have to keep taking money for five years or until you reach age 59½, whichever is longer. That means that if you start annuitizing at age 45, you'll have to take money for 15 years to avoid the penalty. (The IRS has privately ruled that you can build a 3% cost-of-living increase into your annual payouts.)

There are three ways to calculate your withdrawal:

Life Expectancy Method

To use this method, simply divide the balance of your IRA account by your life expectancy or the joint and last survivor expectancy of you and your designated beneficiary. You can recalculate this amount each year, or simply reduce your life expectancy by one for each year you make withdrawals. This method yields the smallest annual payment because it doesn't consider future earnings in the account.

Let's say that you're 50 years old and your IRA balance is $100,000. Your life expectancy is 33.1 years. You may withdraw $3,021.15 without penalty.

Amortization Method

To use this method, amortize your IRA like a mortgage (using your single life expectancy or the joint and last survivor life expectancy of you and your designated beneficiary) and a reasonable long-term interest rate. This method yields larger withdrawals because it includes future earnings in the account (the interest rate selected).

Let's say that you're 50 years old, your IRA balance is $100,000, and you set an 8% interest rate for amortization. $100,000 amortized at 8% for 33.1 years yields $8,679 per year. You may withdraw $8,679 without penalty.

Annuity Factor Method

To use this method, amortize your account balance using insurance mortality tables showing a shorter life expectancy to withdraw a larger amount each year.

If you own your home and you need more money than you can get with the annuitization method, you can combine early withdrawals with a home equity loan to leverage your early withdrawals. Here's how it works: take out a home-equity loan or line of credit and use the annuitization method to pay off the loan with IRA withdrawals. You'll avoid a huge up-front withdrawal and your IRA will continue compounding tax-free. You'll pay ordinary income tax on your annual withdrawals. But the interest you pay on up to $100,000 of your home-equity indebtedness should be tax deductible, offsetting the tax.

Let's assume: 1) you're 50 years old; 2) you have a $100,000 rollover from your 401(k), 3) you've just been downsized from a management position with a large corporation, and 4) you need $50,000 to buy a print shop franchise. If you take out a 10-year home-equity loan at 8%, your annual payments will be $7,279.68. You can easily cover the payments by annuitizing your IRA under the amortization method, above. The bulk of your IRA continues compounding for long-term growth, and you avoid a $5,000 penalty for a $50,000 early withdrawal.

6.4.8 Minimum Distributions

Most employees today take their qualified retirement plan balances in cash, to roll into an IRA for continued tax-deferred growth and flexible withdrawals. Many others have accumulated large accounts from their own investments over time. Most investors will have to face complicated IRA withdrawal rules.

Since IRAs are intended to provide retirement income, you have to start withdrawing money from your regular deductible IRA, nondeductible IRA, or Spousal IRA by April 1 of the year after you reach age 70½. This is called the required beginning date. (Roth IRAs have no required minimum distributions.) Your minimum distribution depends on your account balance and life expectancy. You can certainly withdraw more, but many investors prefer to withdraw the minimum to preserve their principal for longer tax-deferred compounding. There are entire books written on taking money out of IRAs. This discussion will help you anticipate how much taxable income you'll have to withdraw from your accounts.

To calculate your first minimum required distribution, start with the account balance as of December 31 of the year you reach age 70½. Then take your life expectancy (or the joint and last survivor life expectancy of you and your beneficiary), as determined by your ages on your birthdays in the year that *you* reach age 70½. (If your beneficiary is not your spouse, you may treat the beneficiary as being no more than 10 years younger than you, even if the beneficiary is a child or grandchild.) Finally, divide the account balance by the life expectancy. If you have more than one IRA, you have to calculate a required minimum distribution for your combined account balances. However, you can take the required total from a single account.

You have to take your first distribution by April 1 of the year after the year in which you reach age 70½. That distribution counts for the calendar year in which you reach age 70½. You have to take your next distribution by December 31 of the same year. That second distribution is based on the same December 31 account balance, *minus* your first distribution. Let's say that Husband reaches age 70½ on August 1, 1998, and rings out the old year with $100,000 in his IRA. Husband's life expectancy at age 70 is 12.1 years. Husband must withdraw $1/12.1$ of his December 31, 1998, account balance, or $8,264, by April 1, 1999. His December 31, 1999, withdrawal will be based on a $91,736 account balance.

You can also take your required minimum distribution over the *joint* life expectancies of yourself and your designated beneficiary. The process works the same as above, except that you use your joint life expectancy to determine your withdrawals. Let's say that Husband reaches age 70½ on August 1, 1998. Wife turns 68 that same year. They ring out the old year with $100,000 in Husband's IRA. Their joint life expectancy is 19.2 years. Husband has to withdraw $1/19.2$ of his account, or $5,208, by April 1, 1999.

You can choose someone besides your spouse to determine your distributions. But if your non-spouse beneficiary is more than 10 years younger, you have calculate your joint life expectancy as if your designated beneficiary were no more than 10 years younger. This rule is supposed to make sure you use the IRA for your own retirement income, and not for estate planning. (If you have more than one beneficiary, you can calculate separate withdrawal periods for each beneficiary.)

If you wait until the required beginning date to take money from your account, you'll have to take your second minimum distribution by December 31 of the *same* year. This will raise your AGI for figuring deductions and credits, and may bump you into a higher tax bracket. If this will be the case, consider taking your required minimum distribution in the actual year in which you reach age 70½, rather than waiting until the required beginning date.

There are two ways to calculate withdrawals in later years:

- With the straight-line method, you (or you and your beneficiary) subtract one year from your life expectancy for each year. Using the joint life example above, Husband must withdraw $1/19.2$ of his December 31, 1998, account balance by April 1, 1999. He must withdraw $1/18.2$ of his December 31, 1998, account balance (minus the first withdrawal) by December 31, 1999; $1/17.2$ of his December 31, 1999, account balance by December 31, 2000; and so on.

- With the recalculation method, you (or you and your beneficiary) recalculate your life expectancy each year. Using the same example, Husband and Wife have joint life expectancies of 19.2 years in 1998, 18.5 years in 1999, and 17.8 years in 2000. Husband must withdraw $1/19.2$ of his December 31, 1998, account balance by April 1, 1999. He must withdraw $1/18.5$ of his December 31, 1998, account balance (minus the first withdrawal) by December 31, 1999; $1/17.8$ of his December 31, 1999 account balance by December 31, 2000; and so on.

- If you're really ambitious, you can use the straight-line method for one spouse and the recalculation method for the other.

If you don't withdraw the required minimum, you'll owe a penalty equal to 50% of what how much you didn't withdraw. Let's say you're 72 years old. Your IRA balance requires you to take $20,000. If you take just $12,000, you'll owe $3,000 tax on the $6,000 more you should have taken out.

The recalculation method lets you make smaller withdrawals now. This obviously cuts your tax. But the difference isn't dramatic, especially in the early years. And the recalculation method has one big problem if you want to maximize your legacy for your heirs. The year after you die, your life expectancy drops to zero and your heirs owe tax on the entire remaining balance.

Use the following table to calculate life expectancies for purposes of minimum distribution requirements, as well as annuitized payments to avoid the 10% early withdrawal penalty. For joint life expectancies, consult IRS Tables VI and VIA.

Life Expectancies for IRA Withdrawals

Age	Multiple	Age	Multiple	Age	Multiple
41	41.5	61	23.3	81	8.9
42	40.6	62	22.5	82	8.4
43	39.6	63	21.6	83	7.9
44	38.7	64	20.8	84	7.4
45	37.7	65	20.0	85	6.9
46	36.8	66	19.2	86	6.5
47	35.9	67	18.4	87	6.1
48	34.9	68	17.6	88	5.7
49	34.0	69	16.8	89	5.3
50	33.1	70	16.0	90	5.0
51	32.2	71	15.3	91	4.7
52	31.3	72	14.6	92	4.4
53	30.4	73	13.9	93	4.1
54	29.5	74	13.2	94	3.9
55	28.6	75	12.5	95	3.7
56	27.7	76	11.9	96	3.4
57	26.8	77	11.2	97	3.2
58	25.9	78	10.6	98	3.0
59	25.0	79	10.0	99	2.8
60	24.2	80	9.5	100	2.7

6.5 Social Security

Our discussion of retirement plans is an appropriate place to discuss strategies for avoiding tax on Social Security benefits. It's cynically fashionable these days to mock Social Security as a dinosaur, a relic of big government doomed to death under an onslaught of aging baby boomers. A recent survey by the New Millennium Foundation found that more Generation X-ers, born in the years immediately following the baby boom, believe in UFOs than believe they will ever see a dime of Social

Security. But, despite the doom and gloom, the hand wringing, and the election-year posturing, Social Security is in better shape than most of its critics realize. Just four changes can assure solvency for most of the next century:

- Raise the retirement age and index it to rising life expectancy.
- Include certain state and local government employees still not covered by the system.
- Raise the Social Security wage base from its current level ($76,200 for 2000, indexed for inflation) to somewhere around $90,000.
- Tax all benefits paid to recipients once they have recovered their original contributions.

I'll give you two good why Social Security won't disappear: 1) old people vote; and 2) Congress knows it. The reality is, Social Security remains an important part of most retirees' income. The Social Security Administration reports that in 1999, the average benefit is $9,360 per year and comprises over half of the average beneficiary's income. That amount won't make most investors rich. But, why pay tax at all if you don't have to?

Social Security itself generally isn't taxable until your provisional income tops certain levels. Provisional income includes regular AGI plus certain adjustments—most notably, municipal bond interest income. If your provisional income clearly tops these thresholds, these steps just make your taxes more complicated. If you're close to the threshold, though, there are strategies you can use to cut your provisional income and preserve your benefits from tax. The answer is to take your income from sources that don't increase your provisional income:

- Immediate annuities pay tax-advantaged income because a portion of each payment consists of return of principal. Only the taxable part of your payment increases your provisional income. (See ***Chapter 7.2.1***, "Immediate Annuities.")

- Fixed and variable annuities grow tax-deferred until you take your gains from the contract. Fixed annuities resemble bank CDs in a tax-deferred wrapper; variable annuities resemble a family of mutual funds, also in a tax-deferred wrapper. But annuity gains don't add to provisional income until you withdraw your gains from the contract.
- Roth IRA distributions are completely tax-free unless you withdraw funds before the five-year holding period or age 59½. What's more, Roth IRA distributions don't increase your provisional income. This makes Roth IRAs more valuable than regular IRAs if your provisional income is near the tax threshold. It can also make sense to convert some or all of your regular IRA to a Roth IRA, even if the income spike in the year you convert subjects all of that year's benefits to tax. For more information, see the discussion of Roth IRAs, above.
- You can draw income from a home equity line of credit, reverse mortgage, or margin account without realizing taxable income. The interest you pay may be less than the tax on Social Security you would pay.
- Low-income housing tax credits boost your spendable income without increasing provisional income. (See ***Chapter 3.***)
- Rental real estate may generate cash flow sheltered by depreciation deductions.

If you're income is right on the edge at the end of the year, considering liquidating principal or using the strategies for avoiding tax on capital gains rather than drawing taxable income that pushes your modified AGI over the threshold.

Chapter 7

Life Insurance and Annuities

Life insurance and annuities are two sides of the same financial coin. Life insurance protects you from dying too soon and leaving your dependents without your support. Annuities protect you from living too long and outlasting your money.

Life insurance and annuities offer two other benefits that few investments can match: state guarantees and asset protection. Each state operates a life insurance guaranty fund, similar to the Federal Deposit Insurance Corporation, that protects policyholders from insurance company failure. Most states protect up to $100,000 of cash value and $300,000 of death benefit. And most states protect life insurance and annuity cash values from certain creditor claims, usually up to $100,000. This protection isn't bulletproof. For example, if you're a doctor and you lose a malpractice suit, you can't just stash your fortune in an annuity. The transfer would be attacked as a fraudulent conveyance. But it's an extra benefit for entrepreneurs and high-risk professionals.

You'll need to do one more chore before choosing a life insurer, and that's to research your potential insurer's credit rating. In the 1980s, several high-flying insurers, including Executive Life, Mutual Benefit, and Baldwin-United, collapsed, forcing policyholders to wait years for the return of their money. But there's no shortage of organizations that rate life insurers for capital strength and claims-paying ability. These include A.M. Best, Standard & Poor's, Moody's, Duff & Phelps, and Weiss Research. Different ratings agencies use different scales to rate companies—Weiss's "A+", their highest rating, goes to just a handful of companies, while Best's A+, their second-highest rating, goes to over 150. But ratings are an important consideration before you buy. You should find at least one at your public library.

These ratings are most important for money you place in the company's fixed accounts. That's because these funds are backed by the insurer's general account, which is subject to all of the company's creditors. It's less important for money you place in variable life and variable annuity subaccounts. That's because these funds are invested in the company's separate accounts, maintained exclusively for the benefit of policyholders. There's no risk that separate account assets can be diverted to satisfy outside obligations. However, a company's claims-paying ability still affects its ability to pay a death benefit.

Finally, you can exchange life insurance and annuity contracts tax-free with a 1035 exchange, named for the section of the tax code that allows it. You can exchange a life policy for a life policy, an annuity for an annuity, and a life policy for an annuity. (You can't exchange an annuity for a life policy.) This is useful if you wish to consolidate accounts, switch to a more successful investment manager, or update older fixed annuities and whole life policies to variable contracts.

7.1 Life Insurance Basics

Life insurance companies tell their agents never to sell life insurance as an investment. I'll respect that and refer to it as a financial tool. The fact is, life insurance can be a terrific tax shelter, and if more investors knew just how to use it, they'd be asking how much they could get their hands on. But life insurance is a complicated purchase, and there are several conditions to satisfy before you buy. First, you should need the death protection, either to protect your family from the loss of your income or to protect your estate from taxes. Second, you should be healthy enough to qualify. Third, you'll need to do some homework to determine which policy is best for you. Fourth, life insurance policies have long surrender periods that limit your ability to withdraw funds during the first few years that the contract is in force. Still, when you've finished reading this Chapter, you'll probably want to call your agent.

Term life is pure death protection, with no investment element. Permanent life combines death protection with an investment account designed to build cash value to help pay premiums down the road. Permanent life offers three strong tax advantages for investors who actually need the death protection: tax-deferred growth, tax-free death benefit, and tax-free income:

- Your cash value grows tax-deferred, just like in an IRA or qualified retirement plan. There's no upfront deduction, of course, but your gain isn't taxed unless you let the policy lapse and cash out for more than you paid in. Your gain, or profit, equals your cash value minus premiums paid.
- When you die, your beneficiary receives the death benefit without paying income tax. Some policies let terminally ill insureds take accelerated benefits for payment of final expenses. These benefits are tax-free. Also, some states allow terminally ill patients to sell their death benefits in viatical settlements. These are also tax-free. Proceeds may be included in the value of your estate, but there are ways to avoid that tax bite, too. (See *Chapter 7.1.2*, "Life Insurance Trusts.")
- You can take money out of the policy, tax-free, by withdrawing your original premiums and borrowing against the rest of the cash value. When you borrow from the policy, the insurance company will charge you interest, but it will credit the policy with earnings as well. Many policies offer wash loan provisions that cut your effective interest rate to zero.

At the same time, there are two important considerations to keep in mind before buying life insurance. Insurance can be expensive, especially if you're in poor health or enjoy death-defying hobbies, like scuba diving or parachuting. Underwriting, which is the decision to accept, reject, or charge an additional premium for a particular policy, makes a big difference in the price you pay. Commissions and mortality charges reduce your actual investment. And if the policy lapses, you'll owe tax on any gain above your cumulative premiums paid. Your policy will lapse if there's not enough cash value to pay the continuing insurance costs. This can happen if you don't pay enough premiums, or if your cash value investments don't perform. To keep the policy from lapsing, add more premium dollars. You can also buy a no-lapse rider protecting the policy from poor investment results. If you no longer need or want the death benefit, you can exchange the policy for an annuity. This will preserve your tax deferral.

For more information, see a life insurance agent or financial planner. Choose one who can place your business with several different carriers. Life insurance prices vary from company to company, even for the same amount of coverage. And premium alone isn't an accurate measure of price. You have to consider cash value growth as well. In November 1997, *Investment Advisor* magazine presented a survey of 31 variable universal life providers. They asked these insurers to project target premiums and 10-year cash values for a 45-year-old nonsmoker, assuming paid-up premiums and a 10% annual investment return. Target premiums ranged from $788 to $2,978, while cash values after 10 years ranged from $5,518 to $33,129. The lowest target premium doesn't necessarily indicate the best value. And a policy without enough cash value is more likely to blow up and require more money in case the investments fail to perform.

In the 1970s, when universal and variable life appeared on the market, tax rates ranged as high as 70%. Since life insurance let investors earn market rates on their investments without current income tax, life insurance became a tremendously popular tax shelter. Single-premium life became especially popular, with a single up-front payment that guaranteed coverage for life and sheltered the entire cash value from taxes as long as the policyholder lived. In 1988, Congress created a seven-pay test to weed out perceived abuses. This test is supposed to make sure that investors use the tax break to buy appropriate amounts of insurance, not merely shelter investment income.

To calculate the seven-pay limit, your agent calculates how much money is needed to fully fund the policy, for life, at any point in the policy's first seven years. This amount is called the seven-pay premium. Then, if at any point in that seven-year period the cumulative premiums paid into the policy exceeds the seven-pay premium, the policy becomes a modified endowment contract, or MEC, and loses much of its tax advantage. Loans and withdrawals will be taxed as ordinary income, up to the amount of gain in the contract. (Death proceeds will remain income tax free.) As coverage limits increase, so do MEC limits. This makes sense, since it takes increasingly larger amounts of cash to fund increasingly larger policies. Naturally, single-premium policies are snared in the trap, since they're paid up from day one.

MEC rules are some of the most complicated in the tax code. Existing policies are grandfathered, unless the death benefit is raised or lowered, and there are all sorts of traps for unwary buyers. Since the seven-pay premium varies according to your age, health, and policy size, there's no easy way to calculate your limit. For more information, see your agent.

7.1.1 Which Policy Is Best For You?

Once you've decided how much insurance you need, it's time to decide what type of policy you want. Here's how the various types of policies work.

Term Life

Term life is pure death protection, with no investment element. You pay your premium. If you die, you collect (well, your beneficiaries do). If you live, your premium dollars go to pay off the poor schmucks that die. Some agents consider term insurance a waste of money since you don't collect if you don't die. If you believe that fire insurance is a waste of money when your house doesn't burn down, then by all means believe it yourself.

Term is appropriate if you need a specific death benefit for a specific period of time. As you grow older, it becomes more and more expensive. If you have a permanent need for insurance, consider one of the permanent life policies below.

Whole Life

Whole life is the traditional form of cash value life insurance. You pay a flat or increasing premium each year. Some of your premium goes directly towards paying for death protection. The rest goes into an investment fund and builds cash value. At some point, the cash value could grow large enough to pay the premium all by itself. At that point, you can keep your coverage without paying a premium.

With most whole life policies, the company invests the cash value for you, and guarantees a minimum investment return comparable to a bank CD or similarly conservative fixed-income investment. The company bears the risk if the investment return isn't enough to keep the coverage in force. The company will usually pass on some of the windfall if investment returns are greater than projected. This windfall is called a dividend. It's actually a return of your premium, and not a traditional dividend you'd earn with a stock or mutual fund. (Life insurance dividends aren't taxed as income so long as the total amount of dividends paid out does not exceed the total amount of premiums you've paid into the policy.) You can take the dividend in cash, use it to reduce your premium, or buy more coverage.

Whole life is best for if you want permanent coverage with predictable premiums and strong guarantees.

Universal Life

Universal life enjoys the same tax advantages as whole life, but with two significant differences that made it a success. First, universal life pays a variable rate depending on current interest rates. Second, universal life gives the policyholder the flexibility to pay whatever premium he or she likes, including nothing at all, as long as there's sufficient cash value to keep the policy in force.

Universal life lost some credibility in the late 1970s and early 1980s. Many agents sold the policies based on projections that high current interest rates would last well into the future. This would quickly build enough cash value to vanish current premiums. Of course, interest rates soon dropped. Thousands of policyholders were forced to pay huge extra premiums into supposedly paid-up policies, or lose their coverage. Some insurers are still suffering from fines and refunds paid to buyers. Universal life is an attractive option for buyers seeking flexibility and healthy current interest rates. Just make sure you buy based on reasonable long-term interest projections.

Variable Life

Strictly speaking, variable life isn't a type of life insurance. Instead, it's a way of investing your policy's cash accumulation value. Variable life extends life insurance's tax-advantaged wrapper to the stock market and other investment markets. You, as policyholder, choose where to invest your cash value among a set of investment subaccounts, just like with mutual funds and variable annuities. There is as nearly as wide a choice of insurance subaccounts as there is mutual funds. In fact, many life insurance subaccounts are clones of popular mutual funds. Life insurers have allied with top mutual fund managers, so it's not unusual to find portfolios from a dozen managers in a single life insurance or annuity contract.

Variable life is available as variable ordinary life, with fixed premiums like traditional whole life, and variable universal life, with the same flexible premium option as universal life. It can be a tremendous tool if you use it properly. You can accumulate cash for college and retirement and guarantee that cash will be available if you die too soon. If you need money before age 59½, you'll avoid a 10% penalty tax on early withdrawals from IRAs and annuities.

Variable life should offer the highest returns over time. However, if your investments don't perform, you'll have to add money to feed the policy. This is especially important if your cumulative withdrawals top your cumulative premiums. Remember, if you let the policy lapse, you'll owe tax on your cumulative gain.

Lots of advisors discourage investors from buying permanent life. Rather than mixing death protection and investments, they recommend you buy inexpensive term coverage and invest the difference outside your life insurance. This way, you avoid paying life insurance commissions on investment dollars. This advice made more sense when conservative whole life was the only life insurance investment choice. But today's variable products can earn the same high returns as mutual funds and other investments. When you add in the life insurance's tax advantages, the case for permanent insurance can be compelling for buyers who truly need the insurance protection.

7.1.2 Life Insurance Trusts

Most investors want to leave at least some sort of financial legacy for their family. An irrevocable life insurance trust, or ILIT, can help guarantee that legacy, as well as serve as a shield against taxes. A trust is an arrangement in which one person, called the grantor, conveys an interest in property, called the trust corpus, to another person, called the trustee, for benefit of a final person or persons, called beneficiaries. An ILIT is an irrevocable trust designed to hold life insurance on the life of the grantor. Briefly, here's how it works:

- The first step is to establish the trust itself and designate the beneficiaries. These can be named individuals, or an entire class of people, such as your grandchildren.
- The next step is for the trustee to apply for life on the grantor or grantors. Most trusts for beneficiaries of married couples buy second-to-die, or survivorship, life insurance. This is coverage that insures two lives and pays at the death of the second, or survivor. They choose this arrangement because estate taxes aren't due until the second death.
- You as the grantor can also transfer existing policies into a new trust. The policy's cash value at the time of the transfer will be the value of the gift for purposes of qualifying for the $10,000 annual exclusion. However, if you transfer an existing policy, you'll have to live for at least three years following the transfer to avoid estate tax on the proceeds. If you die within the three-year period, the transfer will be treated as a gift in contemplation of death and the proceeds will be included in your estate.
- The grantor cannot retain any incidents of ownership. This means that you cannot retain any interest in the trust income or principal, change the beneficiary, surrender or cancel the policy, assign it or revoke an assignment, pledge it for a policy loan, or obtain a policy loan. If you

retain any of these incidents of ownership, the proceeds will be taxed in your estate and you will lose the advantage of trust ownership.

- You can draft the trust document to let the trustee use trust assets to benefit your spouse (if the trust asset is a single-life policy) or your beneficiaries (if the trust asset is a joint-life policy). This lets you use trust assets for retirement income or family support. However, the trustee can't use trust assets for the benefit of the grantor without blowing the estate-tax exemption.

- Each year, as you make gifts to the trust, you have to give the beneficiaries the power to withdraw their share of the annual gift from the trust. This is called a *Crummey* power, named for the case that established this point of law, and it's necessary to qualify your gift to the trust as a complete gift and avoid including the proceeds in your estate at your death. Gifts to the trust may be taxable if they top $10,000 per donor per recipient. Let's say that you and your spouse establish an ILIT for the benefit of your three children. You can give the trust up to $60,000 per year, equal to $10,000 from each of you to each of the three beneficiaries.

At your death (or your survivor's death, in the case of second-to-die coverage), the trust receives the insurance proceeds, income- and estate tax free. At that point, the trustee can buy illiquid assets, such as real estate or a business, from the estate to provide cash to pay taxes. Or, the trustee can simply distribute the proceeds of the policy to the beneficiaries according to the terms of the trust.

A life insurance trust may be a good place to put excess assets that you don't need to fund your current standard of living. Transferring assets into an ILIT will reduce your taxable estate by the amount of the transfer, plus any income those assets would have earned during your life. For most investors, the hard part can be finding excess assets to fund the trust. Here are some suggestions:

- You can use a margin loan to borrow against your stocks or other securities.
- You can use a home equity loan or reverse mortgage to borrow against your home. (Ordinarily, there's no interest deduction for home-equity proceeds you use to buy life insurance. In this case, though, you're giving the loan proceeds to the trust, which then buys the insurance. This preserves your interest deduction.) This converts a taxable asset—the value of your home—into a tax-free asset, life insurance proceeds.
- You can liquidate assets to pay premium dollars with principal, not just income, secure in the knowledge that the insurance proceeds will replace the value of the lost assets for your heirs.

7.2   Annuity Basics

An annuity is a contract with a life insurance company that lets you take a guaranteed income for life. Annuities are designed as insurance against outliving your income. You can invest that portion of your portfolio, without ever having to whether it will last.

Annuities are defined by three main characteristics:

- An immediate annuity begins paying an income immediately, while a deferred annuity accumulates earnings over time.
- A single premium annuity lets you make a single investment. A flexible premium annuity lets you make flexible investments over time.
- Finally, a fixed annuity pays a fixed interest rate over time, while a variable annuity ties your return to some underlying variable investment.

Any annuity is a combination of these three choices: a flexible-premium deferred variable annuity, perhaps, or a single premium fixed immediate annuity.

Annuity buyers need to consider the same credit ratings issues as insurance buyers. This is especially true with immediate annuities, fixed annuities, and variable annuity subaccounts. Variable annuity subaccounts are held in separate accounts for the benefit of the contract holders; however, general credit issues may affect an insurer's ability to pay a guaranteed death benefit in the event the contract holder's subaccounts suffer actual losses.

7.2.1 Immediate Annuities

Immediate annuities offer immediate income for a term as long as your life. The main attraction is an income you can't outlive. That makes them tremendously powerful retirement income choices. Payout periods can range from a period of years to a joint lifetime, with optional period-certain guarantees to protect your heirs if you drop dead after getting a single payment. Immediate annuities are a surprisingly underappreciated choice for income investors. As life expectancies rise and retirements lengthen, we should see more and more investors choose to annuitize.

When you buy an immediate annuity, the company takes your life expectancy (or the payout term) and its own current interest rate to determine an income it can pay over the course of your life. The process works like amortizing a mortgage in reverse. But the company guarantees that it will pay the income no matter how long you live. Immediate annuities are often described as a gamble—with you betting against the company that you'll outlive your life expectancy. In fact, immediate annuities are the exact *opposite* of a gamble. They let you shift the risk of outliving your money to the company.

Here are the basic tax rules for immediate annuities:

- Income from an immediate annuity is partially tax-free. That's because a portion of each payment is a return of your own principal. To determine the exclusion ratio, or tax-free portion of the payment, first determine your investment in the contract. This will be your cost, minus the value of any refund feature. Next, divide that investment into the total income you expect to earn from the contract. Finally, multiply this percentage by the amount of each payment. Your result will be the tax-free portion of each payment. Your annuity provider will report the taxable part of each year's income on Form 1099-R at the end of the year. When your original investment is completely paid out, your remaining payments are fully taxable.
- If you die before you recover your cost, you can deduct your unrecovered cost on your final tax return. (Well, your executor can.) This is a miscellaneous itemized deduction *not* subject to the 2% floor.
- The longer you wait, the more income you get for each dollar of original contribution. This is because your life expectancy shrinks. The less time the insurance company has to pay out your income, the more it can give you now with every payment.
- Depending on state law, immediate annuities can also help protect your assets if you or your spouse accept Medicaid for nursing home costs. Medicaid rules require you to spend all but a specified portion of your assets on nursing home costs before the state steps in to pick up the tab. Immediate annuities let you convert a portion of those assets into an income stream that Medicaid can't take. This is a tricky, constantly changing area. Consult a qualified expert before making any specific moves.

Traditionally, immediate annuities have offered fixed payments for life. These plain vanilla payouts grow less valuable over time as inflation eats away at your purchasing power. But a new breed of variable immediate annuity has expanded retirement income options. These contracts pay out a fixed number of accumulation units whose value will fluctuate with the value of the underlying investment. Let's say that your contract includes 1,000 accumulation units worth $100 each. The insurance company might promise to pay out four units per month. The first month, you'll get $400. If the value of the accumulation units rises to $105 by the second month, you'll get $420. So, rather than accepting the insurance company's own declared interest rate, your income over time can rise or fall with the value of the underlying accumulation units. Some contracts let you choose multiple settlement options, such as putting 50% into a fixed payout and 50% into a variable payout. Others let you borrow or withdraw any remaining unpaid principal.

Impaired risk annuities are an attractive for investors with poor health. Immediate annuities have traditionally been based on published life expectancies. This made them a lousy choice for unhealthy and terminally ill prospects. Impaired risk annuities use underwriting methods to more accurately determine a buyer's true life expectancy. Shorter life expectancies make for larger payments. This lets buyers guarantee a larger income, or buy the same income for less money up front.

Immediate annuities are terrific alternatives to bonds for investors seeking current income. Remember, most money market funds, bonds, and bond funds are inefficient. That's because the bulk of your total return comes in the form of immediately taxable income. Buying an immediate annuity lets you take the bulk of your income in the form of tax-free return of principal. You can then invest the rest of your principal in more efficient investments, further cutting you tax bill.

7.2.2 Fixed Annuities

A fixed annuity resembles a bank CD in a tax-deferred wrapper. The insurance company guarantees a fixed interest rate for a specified period of time. At the end of that period, the company renews the contract for a new period at a new rate. Fixed annuities are a popular choice for older, conservative investors who don't need current income. They're also popular estate-planning choices for investors looking to bypass probate.

Fixed annuities carry no up-front sales loads or commissions. Instead, the company levies a contingent deferred sales charge on withdrawals within a specified period, much like the familiar penalty for early withdrawal you'd face with a bank CD. Surrender periods range from as low as four years to as long as 12. Actual charges range from 4% to 12%. Most companies will let you withdraw 10% of the contract value or 100% of the annual earnings without penalty. There may also be a market value adjustment on withdrawals within a specified period to protect the company from the effect of interest rate changes during the contract term.

Shop around before you buy a fixed annuity. Most companies offer one-time interest bonuses and teaser rates. These up-front incentives occasionally mask unreasonably high and long surrender charges. The agent's commission can sometimes be more than your first year's income. And make sure you buy from a strong company. Fixed annuity assets are held as a part of the company's general asset account. So, the company's credit rating is a crucial consideration.

If you like the thought of a tax-deferred CD, but don't like the long surrender periods of some contracts, consider a variable annuity instead. Variable annuities have lower commissions, lower expenses, and shorter surrender periods than their fixed counterparts. But variable annuities almost always offer a fixed account option similar to a fixed annuity. And variable annuities let you switch your money, tax-free, into other investments if rates drop. Variable annuities also offer money market and bond subaccounts that may be appropriate for fixed annuity investors.

7.2.3 Variable Annuities

A variable annuity is a contract with an insurance company that offers a family of investment subaccounts. It resembles a mutual fund family in a tax-deferred wrapper. In fact, many variable annuity investment subaccounts are clones of popular mutual funds. Variable annuities offer anywhere from a dozen to more than 100 subaccounts, sometimes from dozens of fund managers. You'll find a fixed account, a money market account, and various stock and bond accounts. Your investment buys accumulation units in one or more of these subaccounts. You can transfer amounts from subaccount to subaccount, usually as often as you wish. During this accumulation period, your money grows tax-deferred. When you're ready to take your money, you can withdraw any number of accumulation units in cash. Or, you can convert the entire contract to an income stream.

There are two main differences between a variable annuity and a regular fund family. First, the variable annuity guaranteed a minimum death benefit to protect your heirs against market downturns. (Some contracts guarantee you'll receive your original contributions, minus any withdrawals. Others raise the death benefit by a certain percentage each year, or reset it at each year's high water mark as you account balance grows.) And second, you have the option to convert your contract into a guaranteed income you can't outlive.

Before we look at the tax advantages and disadvantages, let's discuss how these contracts work:

- There are no up-front commissions with variable annuities.

- Most contracts impose a back-end surrender charge on early contract withdrawals. A typical surrender charge begins at 7% for surrenders during the first contract year, then declines 1% each year until reaching zero in the eighth year. (Most companies will let you withdraw up to 10% of your account balance each year without penalty.) Some contracts impose a "rolling" surrender charge and begin a new surrender period with each deposit.
- The insurer levies an annual "mortality & expense" charge that covers insurance expenses and commissions, plus fund management fees that cover investment management and operating expenses. Together, these fees make up the total expense ratio. No-load annuities naturally sport lower expense ratios because there's no commission to pay.
- When you contribute to the contract and transfer money between subaccounts, you buy and sell "accumulation units" priced according to the net asset value of the particular subaccounts involved.
- Many contracts provide optional riders such as nursing home and disability waivers, which let you withdraw money without normal surrender charges. Some newer contracts even offer "Chinese menus" that let you pick and choose the riders you want. Your choices then determine the fees you pay for the contract.
- You can usually find tools such as portfolio rebalancing and dollar-cost averaging.
- Annuity account balances are protected from creditors. In some states, annuity payments are also protected. This can make annuities effective asset protection tools.
- Some variable annuities offer a "bonus" of around 4% on all deposits. The unstated purpose of the bonus is to make up the surrender penalty from moving out of an older annuity. But be careful here. The bonus has to come out of somebody's pocket—and you already know that it's yours. Bonus annuities generally have higher expenses and longer surrender periods than comparable contracts without the bonus. And the bonus may be erased at your premature death. The Securities and

Exchange Commission (SEC) has just announced an investigation into bonus annuity marketing practices. Presumably, they're looking to make sure that issuers aren't using the bonus to "twist" purchasers out of old contracts when there's no other benefit to moving.

Variable annuities offer several tax advantages over comparable mutual funds and even qualified retirement plans:

- Your earnings grow tax-deferred until you withdraw money from the contract.
- You can transfer money from one subaccount to another without paying tax on your gains.
- You can invest as much as you want no matter how much you make. There are no contribution limits or income eligibility limits as there are with qualified plans or IRAs. This makes them obvious places for supplemental retirement savings after you've exhausted your qualified plan.

These advantages offer obvious appeal. And this appeal has made variable annuities the insurance industry's biggest seller. At the same time, annuities carry several tax disadvantages. If you're not careful, these disadvantages can wipe out the benefit of tax deferral:

- Withdrawals are taxed as income first until you've withdrawn your entire gain. By contrast, when you sell mutual fund shares, part of your proceeds consist of your basis in the shares. You can also borrow against taxable funds for tax-free cash.
- All gains are taxed as ordinary income. There's no opportunity to profit from lower long-term gain rates as there is with taxable funds.
- There is usually a 10% penalty for withdrawals before age 59½. The main exceptions are for payments to a beneficiary, payments due to disability, and payments you take when you annuitize the contract.

- There's no stepped-up basis for gains at death as there is for taxable funds. Your beneficiaries will owe ordinary income tax, at their rate, on any gain they take from the contract. They have five years from the date of your death to withdraw gains and pay tax. (They can take a deduction for any estate tax attributable to the annuity account values included in your estate.)

We've seen that you have two main strategies for cutting tax on your investments: paying less and paying later. Variable annuities let you pay later, at the expense of paying less. And variable annuities are more expensive than comparable mutual funds. The question is, which is better for you? Does the tax deferral you get from an annuity outweigh the lower fees and favorable long-term capital gains treatment you get from a taxable fund? This question is particularly important since the Taxpayer Relief Act of 1997 cut capital gains rates. It's even more important if you're looking at a fund that's available as a taxable mutual fund and an annuity subaccount.

The National Association of Variable Annuities (NAVA), an industry trade group, commissioned the accounting firm of Price Waterhouse to study whether variable annuities still make sense after the Taxpayer Relief Act of 1997. The study assumed certain facts that may or may not apply in your case: specifically, a 28% tax rate during the accumulation phase, a 15% rate during the withdrawal phase, 20% portfolio turnover each year, and an extra 0.87% annual fee for annuities. They study concluded that variable annuities remain attractive retirement savings tool, even after the new, lower capital gains rates. But the real issue isn't whether they work under NAVA's assumptions. The real issue is whether they work for you. Here are five questions to ask before you buy a variable annuity:

Do you need retirement savings?

Variable annuity gains don't qualify for stepped-up basis at your death. And contract values are included in your taxable estate. Don't use an annuity to shelter gains you plan to leave to your heirs. You can buy taxable funds to qualify for stepped-up basis at your death. You can buy variable life insurance to take tax-free income in the form of policy loans. Or, you can set up an irrevocable life insurance trust to exclude assets from your taxable estate.

The NAVA study didn't specifically examine the tax consequences of annuity balances at death. This is a serious omission. If your estate is large enough to be subject to estate tax ($675,000 in 2000), you should buy taxable funds.

Are you maxing out your retirement plans and IRAs?

Qualified plans give you up-front tax deductions, plus a possible employer match. Unless your plan is funded with annuities, there are no insurance expenses. So don't even think of making ongoing annuity contributions with money you can contribute to your retirement plan, IRA, or Roth IRA.

Don't buy a variable annuity in an IRA if you don't want the guaranteed death benefit or annuity purchase option. Why pay for them if you won't use them?

Do you need tax deferral?

Remember the Three Commandments of Tax-Efficient Investing from Chapter 1.4? (If not, they're 1) it's what you *keep* that counts; 2) once you've decided what to buy, find the most tax-efficient way to buy it; and 3) never make an investment decision *solely* for tax reasons.) You need to remember all of these rules when considering a variable annuity. A variable annuity isn't an investment as much as it is a wrapper for holding investments. Once you've decided you need supplemental retirement savings, *first* decide how you're going to invest. *Then* decide whether they belong inside a variable annuity.

Not all of your investments benefit from tax deferral. We've already seen that tax deferral is most valuable for sheltering current income, taxable today at ordinary rates. It's less valuable for sheltering capital gains, taxable tomorrow at lower rates. (This is especially true if your taxable alternative is a stock index fund. You can't live long enough for an annuity's tax deferral to outweigh the index fund's lower expenses and tax efficiency.) Variable annuities are best suited for cash, taxable bonds, and dividend-paying stocks like utilities and REITs. They're also good vehicles for inefficient investment strategies like the dogs of the Dow, fund switching, market timing, and portfolio rebalancing. Don't create new tax-deferred accounts if you don't truly need them.

If you plan to annuitize your account someday in the future, you have two choices. You can buy taxable investments today, then liquidate them to buy an annuity tomorrow. But liquidating them can cost you a bundle in commissions and taxes. Or you can buy the annuity today, and annuitize later without taking the tax hit. Generally, the more time you have until you annuitize, the more sense it makes to buy the annuity today. Planning to annuitize down the road is one circumstance that calls for buying an annuity regardless of how you plan to invest your account.

A variable annuity can also help hold down your adjusted gross income in order to qualify for breaks such as Roth IRA eligibility, tax credits, or the rental real estate loss allowance. If your investment income regularly disqualifies you for these breaks, an annuity may be your answer.

Is your tax bracket today higher than your tax bracket tomorrow?

This is the hardest question to answer—especially if you still have time until retirement—because you don't know what your tax bracket will be during retirement. You can't assume that your rates will be lower. Plenty of investors who've paid off their houses and packed off the kids find that losing their deductions pushes them into *higher* brackets in retirement.

The NAVA study assumed 28% federal and 6% state tax rates during the accumulation phase, then 15% federal and 6% state tax rates during the payout phase. That's typical for today's annuity owners. (If you're married filing jointly and taking the standard deduction, you'll need to earn more than $55,000 before you hit that 28% federal rate.) But the principle is simple—the greater the difference between today's tax rate and tomorrow's, the more valuable the annuity becomes.

How much will the annuity cost?

Annuities charge a "mortality & expense" fee that pays for the death benefit and the broker's commission. This fee compares similarly to the 12b(1) fee you'll pay to most back-end and level-load funds. But you can avoid it with a no-load fund, index fund, or exchange-traded fund. And there may be other expenses for nursing and disability waivers, stepped-up death benefits, and the like. These extra fees naturally eat into returns. Don't pay them for features you don't want or don't need.

The NAVA study assumed a fund cost of 1.00% per year and an annuity cost of 1.87%. Other studies have reached similar conclusions. 0.87% per year is a small price to pay if you're getting real value from your contract.

Let's put it all together. Consider buying a variable annuity for supplemental retirement savings if:

- You're already maxing out your retirement plans and IRAs
- You plan to spend your account balance during your lifetime, and not leave it to your heirs

- You plan to buy investments that benefit more from tax deferral than tax efficiency
- Your tax bracket today is higher than your likely tax bracket tomorrow
- You can find a well-priced contract with the features you need.

These rules apply for systematic investments over time. If you have a single lump sum of $25,000 or more to invest in equities and the patience to see your investment through the market's usual swings, you're probably better off in a tax-managed mutual fund or tax-efficient separate account.

If you're not happy with an annuity you own today, you're not necessarily stuck with it. You can use a "1035 exchange" to swap it for a new contract with better fund choices, lower fees, or more flexible terms. You have to transfer money from the first contract directly to the second—you can't just surrender your first contract, take the cash, and dump it into the second. There may be a cost to switch if you're still within your existing contract's surrender period. And you'll start a new surrender period with the new contract. Your current provider can quote your surrender charge. It's up to you to decide if the benefits of the new contract outweigh the costs of the switch.

Some annuity providers offer computer programs that purport to calculate exactly which choice is better, funds or annuities. These are like any other financial planning programs based on current assumptions. Tax rates change, expenses and investment results vary, and personal circumstances change. Don't put too much faith into projections based on assumptions you know will change. These programs are most useful when they show truly dramatic differences. If you do choose to crunch the numbers, run several comparisons using different future tax rates to see how changing assumptions affect your results.

Finally, do your homework, just like you would with any other investment. Shop around. Make sure your contract offers experienced investment managers, reasonable expenses, and a fair surrender charge. Also make sure the issuer has a respectable credit rating. These aren't as important with variable annuities as with other insurance products. But, fixed account assets are still a part of the insurer's general assets, and if you annuitize your contract, your income will depend on the company's safety.

7.2.4 Split Annuities

A split annuity is a way to earn tax-advantaged annuity income now, without locking your money up for the future. It involves buying an immediate annuity for current income plus a deferred annuity to return your original investment at the end of a specified time.

Let's say you have $100,000 to invest. You could simply buy a bond for current income. But, you'll owe tax on that income unless you buy a muni bond. A split annuity is a tax-advantaged alternative. As I write this (December 1998), one A+ rated company would let you pay $25,615 for an immediate annuity paying $471.93 per month, or $5,663.16 per year. This represents a 5.66% annual return on your $100,000 total. The remaining $74,385 goes into a fixed annuity paying 7.70% the first year and 5.50% thereafter. At the end of five years, the insurer hands back your original $100,000. With this arrangement, most of your income consists of tax-free return of your original principal. The advantage is that you save what you otherwise would have paid in taxes. The disadvantage is that at the end of the arrangement, $25,615 of your original principal will consist of annuity gain taxable as ordinary income.

7.2.5 Equity Index Annuities

Equity index annuities are a new hybrid of fixed and variable annuities. They offer a return tied to an equity index or a guaranteed return if the index loses money. There are currently more than 100 you can buy. These contracts promise no pain—no chance of actually losing money—but offer little gain compared to what you can make in the market yourself. The main problem with most of these contracts is that your return tracks the S&P 500 Composite Stock *Price* index, which omits dividends. Losing that dividend income costs a tremendous amount over time, as you'll soon see. (Some newer contracts include dividends; others let you choose the index to track. This is a quickly changing area, so it's important to shop around.)

Different companies have different ways of crediting your gains, depending on the participation rate and crediting method. The participation rate tells you what percentage of the index's gain you earn. It's not guaranteed, and it can change as often as monthly. Participation rates usually fall when markets grow more volatile, because the cost of the options contracts the insurance company buys to track the market rises. The crediting method tells you how the company determines the gain itself:

- With the "annual reset" method, the company measures the annual change in the index and resets the starting point each year
- With the "point-to-point" method, the company measures the total change in the index over the life of the entire contract
- With the "high-water" method, the company measures the change from the start of the contract to the highest anniversary value.

The company might promise you something like "90% of the price appreciation of the S&P 500" (determined according to one of the three methods) *or* "3% per year of 90% of the initial investment." The company invests the bulk of your money in its own general account to cover the minimum guaranteed return, then puts the rest into options or futures to capture the index return.

Equity index annuities are taxed like any other annuity. You can invest an unlimited amount; your money grows tax-deferred until withdrawal;

you'll pay tax at ordinary rates when you take out your money; and your heirs will owe gain at their ordinary rate at your death. You can make a 1035 exchange from one equity-index contract to another, or from an equity-index contract to a fixed or variable annuity. These contracts usually carry hefty surrender charges; if you withdraw your money before the end of a specified period, such as five, seven, or nine years, you may be limited to the fixed return floor, regardless of how the index performs in the meantime.

Equity index annuities give you *some* of the index's growth (but not necessarily 100%, and no generally no dividends) or *some* of the fixed guarantee (but not as much as you could earn in a straight fixed annuity). The key here is how you use them. Equity index annuities give you a chance to juice your returns on "safe" money. But they're not a substitute for true equity investments.

One equity-index annuity issuer runs prominent ads soliciting agents to sell their contract. The ads display a standard mountain chart, familiar to anyone who's ever seen a mutual fund ad, showing a hypothetical investor's account growing from $250,000 in April 1982, to $643,373 in April 1996. That *looks* impressive—but, over 14 years, it equals just 6.99% per year. That's less than 7% for a "stock" fund in the greatest bull market in history—less than most bond funds earned for the same period! (By the way, the agent earns a *13.5%* commission. Nothing that pays a 13.5% commission is worth buying.)

7.3 Life Insurance vs. Annuities

Investors have poured hundreds of billions of dollars into variable annuities. In fact, they've become the insurance industry's top-selling product. Just how valuable is tax deferral, especially when it means converting capital gains to ordinary income? Life insurance offers tax deferral too, along with tax-free income and a tax-free death benefit. If you own a variable annuity, and you also need life insurance protection, you may be better off investing your annuity dollars in a variable universal life policy. The difference turns mostly on whether you plan to spend your gains during your lifetime, or leave them to your heirs.

- Annuities don't require underwriting. Life insurance can require extensive underwriting, which can make it too expensive if you're health is poor.
- Annuity contract fees include minimal fees for mortality and insurance expenses. Life insurance includes hefty fees for death benefit coverage—which is why you should use it only if you genuinely need the death benefit.
- Annuities carry a 10% penalty for withdrawals before age 59½. There are fewer exceptions to this rule than there are with IRAs. Life insurance cash values are available at any age without penalty. (Surrender charges may apply in both cases.)
- Annuity withdrawals are taxed as ordinary income until you've drained all your gains. Life insurance loans and withdrawals are tax-free as long as the policy remains in force.
- Annuity gains are taxed to your heirs as ordinary income, at their rates. Life insurance proceeds are nearly always income tax-free to your heirs.
- Annuity values, including gains, are always includible in your estate. Life insurance proceeds are excludible from your estate in a variety of ways. This won't do much for you—but your kids will be happier to see you at Christmas.

Finally, lots of annuity owners who don't need current income from their contracts are realizing that their tax-deferred gain may become a tax time bomb for their beneficiaries, who will owe huge amounts of tax at the owners' deaths. Many of them are trading their annuities for insurance to give their beneficiaries a tax-free death benefit. The main drawback is that they owe tax at the time of the exchange on the accumulated gain in the annuity. If you've bought an annuity, and you aren't likely to need the money, should you exchange the annuity for life insurance?

The answer depends on two factors. First, how much your heirs are likely to receive, after taxes at their marginal rates? Second, how much life insurance you can buy after surrendering your annuity? If your after-tax annuity proceeds can buy you more death benefit, then by all means dump the annuity. You'll do better for your heirs, and you'll be able to tap your account without paying tax.

Let's say that at age 60, you bought an annuity paying 8%. Now you're 69, and the annuity is worth $100,000. Your life expectancy is 12.6 years, and at your death, the annuity is likely to be worth $263,717. Your heirs are in the 28% bracket, so their net inheritance will be $217,876 ($263,717 minus 28% of the $163,717 gain). If you can buy more than $217,876 worth of coverage, your heirs win.

If you don't want to pay the accumulated tax all at once, consider annuitizing the contract and using the tax-advantaged income to buy life insurance. You can give the income to your heirs, use it to buy a policy yourself (if your total estate will be under the unified credit exemption equivalent), or give it to an irrevocable life insurance trust.

About the Author

Edward A. Lyon, JD, is a graduate of Hamilton College and The University of Cincinnati College of Law. He is a tax attorney and former financial consultant for several of America's largest financial services organization. He has appeared on CNN, MSNBC, CNBC, Fox News Network, and even *The Roseanne Show*, which dubbed him "the funniest tax guy in America." For more information, consult his web site at www.taxtuneup.com.

Appendix 1

Write Off Investment Expenses

If Abbie Hoffman were alive today, he would tell you: "Deduct this book!" You might think that by the time you file your tax return, you've done all you can to cut your tax. But there's still one vein left for you to mine. If you're serious enough about your investments to make it this far, you probably read investment guides. You probably subscribe to *Fortune*, *Forbes*, *Money*, or *The Wall Street Journal*. You may have paid a financial planner. You may have bought stock on margin. These are all deductible expenses—right down to the cost of this book. Write off every dollar you spend to manage your money!

Investment expenses you incur to produce taxable income are deductible up to net investment income subject to the 2% floor on miscellaneous itemized deductions. Deductible expenses include:

- Asset management fees you pay to money managers or financial planners
- Legal and accounting fees relating to investments
- Fees for investment advice (fees paid to money managers or financial planners)
- Bookkeeping and secretarial fees relating to investments
- Books and subscriptions relating to investments
- IRA custodial fees, if paid separately from the account
- Account fees for dividend reinvestment plans

- Safe deposit boxes that you use to store investment information
- Investment-related travel (31 cents per mile or actual expenses for travel to and from your broker, trips away from home to meet with investment advisors and manage investment property, etc.) There's no deduction for investment seminars or travel costs for shareholder meetings.
- 50% of investment-related meals and entertainment (lunch with your financial advisor, members of your investment club, and the like)
- Home computer costs for a computer you use to manage your investments. (See *The Dictionary of Tax Deductions* at ***www.taxtuneup.com.***)

Include commissions you pay to buy and sell investments in the cost of the investment for figuring gains and losses when you sell. However, if you pay your broker or investment manager an asset management fee that includes commissions on investment trades, deduct the fee the year you pay.

For more information, see IRS Publication 550, "Investment Income and Expenses."

Appendix 2

Write Off Investment Interest

Interest you pay to buy or hold most taxable investments is deductible, up to your net investment income. If your investment interest exceeds your net investment income—a real possibility in flat or declining markets—you can carry forward the excess against future investment income. Here are the rules:

- "Net investment income" is investment income minus investment expenses.
- "Investment income" includes gross income from property held for investment, such as interest, dividends, royalties, and annuities. It does not include capital gains unless you choose to treat them as investment income. However, if you do so, you'll have to pay tax at ordinary income rates, rather than preferential capital gains rates, on those gains. Investment income also does not include passive activity income.
- Investment expenses are expenses directly related to taxable investments allowable *after* figuring the 2% floor on miscellaneous itemized deductions. Let's say that in 1999, your AGI is $60,000. Your miscellaneous itemized deductions include $1,000 for investment newsletters and other investment expenses, $600 for tax preparation, and $400 in unreimbursed employee business expenses. Your deductible

investment expenses are just $800 ($2,000 in miscellaneous itemized deductions minus 2% of AGI, or $1,200).

- You have to show that you actually use your investment debt to buy or hold taxable investments. You can't simply borrow against your investments to finance personal expenses and deduct the interest, the way you can with home equity interest. Safeguard your investment interest deduction by keeping separate accounts for investment borrowing. Don't use funds from your investment accounts for personal or business expenses.
- There's no deduction for interest that you pay to buy or hold tax-exempt bonds.
- There's no investment interest deduction for interest you use to buy or hold passive activities. Instead, deduct this interest as a business expense to determine net passive income or loss.

Calculate your investment interest deduction on *Form 4952*. Investment interest is *not* subject to the phaseout of itemized deductions for AGIs above $126,600.

www.ingramcontent.com/pod-product-compliance
Lightning Source LLC
Chambersburg PA
CBHW020743180526
45163CB00001B/323